ETIM...

MAINTAIN YOUR WHITE

PURITY FOR THE COOL TEEN IN A SEXUALIZED WORLD

For: Teenagers, Parents and Teen Mentors

MAINTAIN YOUR WHITE
Purity For The Cool Teen In A Sexualized World

Copyright © 2019

ISBN: 978-978-978-629-9

No part of this book may be used without the written permission of the publisher

Published in Nigeria by:

Richville Prints Ltd
Suite GF 02B, UTC Building,
Area 10, Garki-Abuja.
08034536596.

TABLE OF CONTENTS

DEDICATION ii
ACKNOWLEDGMENTS.. iii
INTRODUCTION vi
DEFINITION OF TERMS.. xiv
CHAPTER one — I Almost Did It............................. 1
CHAPTER two — Hey, Friends 7
CHAPTER three Who Is In The Garden? 15
CHAPTER four — Where Do You Hangout? 25
CHAPTER five — Look Inside Your Head 31
CHAPTER six — I Got My Mind Made Up 41
CHAPTER seven — You Think You've Got Talent? 51
CHAPTER eight — Watch Your Back 55
CHAPTER nine — Come Tell Me Why 67
CHAPTER ten Welcome To The White Club 81
CHAPTER eleven— The Three Masquerades.......... 95
CHAPTER twelve — After The Rain............................103
CHAPTER thirteen — How Prepared Are You? 111
CHAPTER fourteen — U-Turn 115
CHAPTER fifteen — Hey, Mom And Dad 119
CONCLUSION 132

DEDICATION

To God Almighty, the Holy One Himself, who saved me early and rescued me from destruction.

To everyone who has decided to embark on this journey of sexual purity. This is for you.

ACKNOWLEDGMENTS.

I am grateful to God for this wisdom, for direction and much mercies. Indeed, I have enjoyed great grace.

To everyone and group that contributed to my choice of sexual purity as a lifestyle, especially my friends from teenage years: Elizabeth, Lade, Grace, Ukeme, Emma N., and Lizzy E. Without your friendship, positive influence and support, I might have gone the wrong path.

My alma-mata: Airforce Girls Military School, Jos, the Fellowship of Christian Students (FCS) and my classmates — "Gamus" for life, indeed!

My fellowship brethren at FECA, I can never stop blessing God for using you to make my late teenage period a blast.

My brother Efa Arikpo, for preaching a message 20 years ago that left a lasting impact on my life. More grace sir.

To my friends, for encouraging me especially as I wrote this book and every time I have a project to execute: Wendy, Enkay, Tina and Terrific Wives. I love you girls.

Acknowledgments

Thank you to my Dad, Dr. Patrick Abang, for showing me the fatherly love which made me not to hunger for boys' own while growing up. And to my Mom, Mrs. Abang, the Apostle of Purposeful Prayer, I am blessed to have you. You uphold me in prayers always. My siblings: Lucy, Joy, Deb, Amba and sis Nora, I love you all.

My spiritual family is the best, headed by my pastors: Pastor Shiyanbade of Living Faith Church, Lokogoma and Pastor Opi Agha of When Women Pray Int'l; I am so grateful to fulfill destiny under both of you.

I specially thank all my mentees worldwide for joining me in this campaign for sexual purity. Teens Roundtable rocks!

I appreciate the Responsible Parents Summit Group for all her prayers and support.

To my PP, Folake, you are such a blessing.

Thank you Richard – the "passion business coach" himself. I celebrate you.

Acknowledgments

To my Editor, Sam Gaza Timothy, thank you for your patience and professional touch on this masterpiece.

Finally, to my darling children, for praying and loving me unrepentantly. And to the husband of my youth, Pastor Matthew Umeh, for helping me on this journey. You have been a solid support and partner in fulfilling purpose. I love you, Sunshine.

INTRODUCTION

Like most children in Nigeria, I grew up with little or no sex education from my parents, teachers, pastors, or even mentors. In fact, thinking of mentors right now is farfetched; the concept didn't exist in my teenage days, at least not in my immediate environment. And when I think of what we heard while growing up as sex education, I can't help but laugh.

Our typical sex education or advice were: "Don't allow any boy touch, shake, or hug you, else you will get pregnant," "When you begin to see your monthly cycle (or period), if you sit close to a boy, you will get pregnant," etc. Ridiculous, right? Well, that's all we got.

Some other parents' approach was to reiteratively threaten to disown their children and send them packing if they ever got pregnant. Parents of boys would threaten that the boy would be compelled to marry the girl they impregnate and end their education from that point. Sex education, few decades ago was majorly about not getting pregnant or putting someone's daughter "in the family way" — a phrase they loved to use.

Introduction

Is this an attempt to blame or berate my parents or the parents of that generation? Not at all. They were simply limited in their knowledge of how to do better. It was the information available, or the lack of it, that resulted to that. At the time, we didn't have access to information like you – the 21st Century teenagers – have. Thus, you have no excuse not to know all you need to know about Sex and Purity.

Enough of relying on what your friend said or did not say. Your peers usually don't know any better than you do, except for the few who deliberately seek for knowledge or are taught about sex at home. Enough of swallowing what you watched on television, in a music video or movie suggesting what your sexuality should be like. Those aren't reliable sources. However, I understand, that is perhaps all that you had before now. Thank God you have this book in your hand which will now help you.

Recently, I carried out a research on about 500 teenagers across several states in Nigeria on why teens have sex before marriage, and this is the summary of the responses I got:

Introduction

Ignorance	—55%
Peer Pressure	—15%
Faulty Mindset	—12%
Identity Crisis	—10%
Puberty (raging emotions)	—8%

This goes to show that the predominant reason teens have sex before marriage is Ignorance. That is why I wrote this book – to supply you with apt knowledge! It was crafted to give you the appropriate knowledge and information about living a life of sexual purity, so you can make the right choices for yourself.

In this book, I would share the story of my own journey to healthy sexuality as a teenager. Trust me, it wasn't easy then, and I am not going to bamboozle you. So, this is not about shoving some commands down your throat. No. Rather, it is you allowing me to help you go through your own process. And letting you know that sexual purity is possible, if you want it. Really you should! I'll show you why, as you read on.

As a teenager, you are at a stage of your life called "Trial Independence". That is, you are seeking to develop your own identity, personality, values, belief system,

Introduction

etc. In other words, you are trying to find YOU. During this period, you especially hear the words 'sex' and 'sexuality' over and over again.

Sex is one word that is greatly misunderstood and misused today because the world, society and culture are bombarding you with messages that are totally different from what God, who is the originator of sex and marriage, intended. As such, they leave you more confused than they met you. True?

The danger of your ignorance of what the consequences of engaging in illicit sexual interactions are is that it will cause you otherwise avoidable pain, regret, and a life of sorrow. Following the trends, lies and misconceptions around sex will not exempt you from the consequences that arise from the poor choices you make. It's time to be wise; to *"borrow sense,"* as the saying goes in Nigeria!

I usually don't like to emphasize how pregnancy or HIV are consequences of premarital sex, because that's only two of many consequences.

Introduction

There are other consequences which you should know about. They will all be discussed in this book. Having said that, a startling statistic reveals that in Nigeria, the incidences of teenage pregnancy are unacceptably high. Unfortunately, due to religious and cultural sensitivities, most Nigerians live in denial of just how common teenage sex is. The glaring reality was revealed by the Demographic Health Survey (DHS) in 2013, which showed that:

- 54% of teenagers had sex before 18 years old
- Only 3 out of 10 women had their first sex later than 20, i.e. 7 out of 10 had sex before 20
- 24% of teenagers had sex before 15 years old (girls and boys)[1]

In Nigeria, an estimated 23% of women aged 15-19 years have begun childbearing, of which 17% have had their first child and 5% are pregnant with their first child. The report shows disparities within the geopolitical zones as follows: Northwest (36%); Northeast (32%); North Central (19%); South-South (12%); Southeast (8%); and Southwest (8%).[2]

Introduction

Furthermore, available data on prevalence of AIDS among young people in Nigeria is put at:

- 2.9% among adolescents aged 15-19 and 3.2% for young people aged 20 to 24
- In 2013, about 160,000 10-19-year-olds lived with AIDS, with an estimated 73,000 being males and 90,000 females
- Young women are more affected by HIV with 3.7% of those aged 20-24 living with HIV compared to 2.4 % among their male counterparts.[3]

Other data by the Nigerian Urban Reproductive Health Initiative showed that no less than 25% of adolescents in Nigeria are having sex already, with 10-15years being the age range for sexual debut.[4]

So, while many (especially parents, the church, and other sane institutions) worry only about pregnancy, sexually transmitted diseases, parental disapproval, delay in accomplishing feats and involvement with other addictions teens face, the 21st Century teenager is engaging in sex at an even earlier age — sadly. Worse still, they don't see anything wrong with it. For them, that's the norm and they have to play the part. Apparently, our priorities have

Introduction

become skewed, and we urgently need to get them straight again.

Thankfully, there is still a percentage that have made a solemn decision to refrain from sex. There are also those who fell in the past but, with better knowledge, have now made the decision to keep themselves until they get married. If you are in either category, or will decide to join after reading this book, then the aim of this book would have been accomplished.

This masterpiece will equip you, arm you, prepare you, and show you the path to keeping your body and marriage bed undefiled ahead. It will help you to live like the Royal Prince or Princess that you are.

Failure to fully understand this complex concept of sexuality is like playing with fire and expecting it not to burn you. Don't believe the lies that say you cannot learn to handle your emotions, control your actions, develop the skills you need to handle your relationships, and establish your sexuality in a healthy way that honors God. You can, darling!

Introduction

Do you see yourself as a king? A queen? Then you must deliberately live like one, and that requires living a life of purity. Or have you ever heard of a worthy king or queen who fornicates on rampage like a street dog? There is a critical association between purity and the palace. Ignore those who say they know people who were not chaste but still arrived at the palace. The question is, as what? There are cooks, waiters, cleaners, etc. in the palace. You need to get there to rule and reign, not as a servant. That is, reaching the fullness of your purpose on earth in grand style. It's time to arise and soar!

Remember,

> Sexual purity is your decision to make. Sexual purity is your responsibility. Sexual purity is possible. Purity is Royalty!

---

[1] https://www.dandc.eu/en/article/nigerias-incidence-teenage-pregnancies-unacceptably-high

[2] https://dhsprogram.com/Who-We-Are/News Room/Teenage-Pregnancy-in-Nigeria-Facts-and-Truth.cfm

[3] https://www.ilo.org/wcmsp5/groups/public/---ed protect/---protrav/---ilo aids/documents/legaldocument/wcms 532857.pdf

[4] https://punchng.com/25 -of- nigerian-adolescents-are-sexually active-nurhi/

DEFINITION OF TERMS

1. Sexual Purity

It is freedom from immorality, especially those of a sexual nature. It is living clean, clear, unmixed, chaste, and uncontaminated with sex-related practices.

Sexual purity is a process. It is not where you begin at; it is where you are going to.

2. Healthy Sexuality

Similar to sexual purity, healthy sexuality is being pure in your thoughts, your words and your actions. It is making conscious effort to ensure that what we see and hear is mostly holy and edifying (First Corinthians ten: thirty-one). It entails purity inwardly and outwardly.

Having a healthy sexuality is a process that involves saying no to temptations, asking and receiving forgiveness from the sin of immorality when we fall, and then making right choices to stay pure afterward.

3. Sex

Sex is intercourse between a male and a female. It involves everything that is or feels sexual in nature, such as kissing, necking, fondling of private parts, actual insertion of organs, etc. More importantly, sex is a joining of two people to become one.

Genesis two: twenty-four says:

> Therefore, a man shall leave his father and mother
> and shall be joined with his wife
> so that they become one flesh.

First Corinthians six: sixteen says:

> There's more to sex than mere skin on skin. Sex is as much spiritual mystery as physical fact. As written in Scripture, "The two become one."

This is why God planned sex to happen only in marriage, so you don't have a piece of yourself here and there by reason of joining yourself with different people through sex. God did not create you to become one flesh with several different people, but with one person only – your future spouse.

Darling, sex is not just physical or biological; sex is spiritual. It was instituted by God as a physical medium to effectuate a spiritual reality. Little wonder the devil has perverted it as a means of thwarting people's destinies. That is, the future greatness God planned for you before you were born gets dwarfed every time you have sex with anyone you are not married to.

Definition of Terms

God wants us to enjoy intimacy and pleasure, so He created a safe place for us to have sex with no spiritual or physical repercussions; and that place is called marriage. Therefore, sex in itself is not bad, neither is it a sin, but it must be done as God planned it (i.e. in Marriage).

4. Virginity

This is a state in which one is said to have never had sexual intercourse. Recently, a new terminology — Secondary Virginity – came to the fore. It is used for people who have had sexual intercourse in the past but have now decided never to have sex again until in marriage.

5. Marriage

The legally or formally recognized union of a man and a woman in a personal, love relationship. Marriage can take place in a customary way, in court or at church. God originated marriage by creating Eve and giving her to Adam as wife. Thus, marriage remains the only place where sex should legitimately take place.

6. Sexualize

To make something sexual in character or quality, or to become aware of sexuality, especially in relation to men and women.

CHAPTER one
I ALMOST DID IT

Growing up, we lived in the staff quarters of the polytechnic where my dad was a senior lecturer. I was lucky, I admit. I came from a good home where my parents provided as much as they could for us. They did well, and I commend them very much. Life in the quarters was more like communal living where children and teens hung out regularly together. It was common to see boys playing football together while the girls strolled up and down, chatting and laughing away. Thinking about it now, I wonder if there really was anything funny to laugh about — but we did anyway. As far as I am concerned, we did that just to get the boys to notice us. Yea, right!

It was in such group meetings that boys talked about which girl they wanted, their escapades with some they already had, etc. In fact, that was where they tabled your matter, as a girl. Boys who had "babes" bragged about it and indirectly pressured those who didn't. Some even got as direct as asking their "babe-less" friends to go "chase" any girl they knew in the neighborhood who was pretty enough and without a boyfriend.

Back then, if you heard loud laughter coming from the boys' corner, it meant either of two things: a boy had just confessed how a girl turned him down or shared how he didn't succeed at taking a girl to bed. Oh, how they would laugh him to scorn! Those boys could jest for Africa. (LOL).

And, if you heard loud cheers and handshakes, he had succeeded; and they would tag him as a "bad guy", fanning his ego. Everyone wanted to be that guy. It was a subtle competition.

I believe it was in one of such gatherings that my case was brought up before "the gods of the land", LOL, because I soon received this long, juicy letter from one of the boys. You know, there were no mobile phones then for calls, chat, or SMS. Thus, the first thing you got from an admirer was a "love letter" delivered mostly through your friend, little sister or brother. He was tall, coffee- brown skinned, and really handsome. I knew him already in the quarters.

In the letter, he called me sweet names, told me how beautiful I was, and how much he loved me. Then he asked me to be his girlfriend.

I was 14years old. I still remember my heart beating so fast that day as I read my first ever love-letter. My emotions raged. So many thoughts flooded my mind And the greatest of all was the feeling that I was the luckiest girl on earth. Could this be a repeat (my own version) of one of the stories I had been reading in the romantic series: Mills and Booms?

I Almost Did It

Let me digress a bit. At the time I was graduating from primary school, I had read all the titles in that series, and soon moved on to the more advanced version called Temptation. I didn't realize what damage I was doing to my mind and mindset at the time. So, it was easy for me to get swept away when "Mr. Tall-Brown-and-Handsome" showed up. This underscores the need for you to watch and guard what kinds of content you feed into your mind. Your mind is the umpire of your life's affairs.

Back to our story, "Mr. Loverman" asked for a reply from me. And, yes, your guess is as good as mine. It was a reverberating 'Yesssssssss!' What else?

Excited as both of us were, we began "dating". He was happy he now had a babe, and I was happy that I was starting to experience what I had only read in books and fantasized about. We would talk unendingly during the holidays and exchange letters during school sessions. I remember hanging around my school mailbox every Friday to read those sweet words of a young man willing to do anything for me. He promised to be my "knight in shiny armour", to protect and care for me. Did I mention that this young man was only 15years old? What could he possibly

I Almost Did It

do for me? (LOL) But what did I care? I was just living my life like a happy teenage girl being loved and in love.

Guess what? My grades began to fall! I, who was best graduating student from primary school started getting the grades of an average student. My focus and attention were divided. Something else had begun sharing my brain with my studies.

After some months, it became boring just talking. Then, one day he took me into his room, brought out a condom and prepared himself to defile me while I lay still like a sheep about to be slaughtered. Till this day, I wonder what my emotions were. Was I scared, anxious, happy, or what? I still can't figure, because I put up no form of resistance whatsoever. After all, he had told me severally that he loved me, so why say a word, right?

Suddenly, a car horn at the gate and his parents are back home. Welcome mom and dad. I wish you knew your little boy is growing fast and flexing his manliness already (I thought to myself). He was just about to take an innocent girl's virginity, but for your unannounced return. But, on a second thought, I believe his parents did that surprise return somewhat deliberately because his mom had this suspicious look on her face. Oh, God bless our mothers for their sensitivity many times!

I Almost Did It

Till this day, I cannot stop thanking God for that divine rescue. Thanks also to my mom whose prayers I believe covered me. I was really naive. I didn't even realize that what was about to happen to me was what the priest in church called fornication. How ignorance is such a terrible thing! (SMH — shaking my head). I have repeatedly professed that I didn't remain a virgin by my power, but solely by God's mercies. As you can see from the foregoing story, I could have easily lost my precious virginity that day, but for God's timely interruption.

Shortly after, I went back to school and, in a meeting with my classmates, I gave my life to Christ at 15 years of age. My God! That was a life-changing experience for me. Suddenly I clearly knew what was wrong and what I needed to do to make amends and to live right. Without anyone telling me, I knew that what my guy and I were toying with was called fornication (a.k.a. fire!); and even though a condom could have held back the sperm, it couldn't have stopped the spiritual joining. Remember, sex is not just physical; it is spiritual.

When I returned home for break, my guy came to show me some *"love"* but was shocked at my resistance. I simply shook my head and stood still. He asked what was happening and I told him I had found Christ and couldn't continue the relationship. Full stop. It was plain and simple. He couldn't believe his ears and I didn't care. My decision was made long before I came home.

I Almost Did It

Chastity isn't about following a bunch of rules so you don't go to hell.

It's about wanting heaven and the person you love.

— Jason Evert

A part of me looked at him and felt some pity when I saw tears fall off his eyes. (Boys can really act drama). But I still held my ground. Yet he didn't believe me. He thought I was joking and tried again some other day, but I stood my ground still. Then he backed off. He didn't even pressure with those words he used when he asked me to be his girl the first time. And that left me wondering: so you let go just like that? But I cared less. Someone more loving and intimate had my attention.

It is my strong opinion that you cannot have a healthy sexuality without being Godly, because you will find yourself going back to doing the wrong things over and over again.

Apostle Paul said in Romans seven: nineteen:I want to do what is good, but I don't. I don't want to do what is wrong, but I do it anyway. But there is hope as Romans six: fourteen says: For sin will have no dominion over you, since you are not under law but under grace. This was when my journey to Sexual Purity began...

CHAPTER two
HEY, FRIENDS

Man is a social being and was created to interact, relate and connect with others. As a teen, there is an even greater need for relationships, friendships.

Isn't it funny that you complain about peer pressure but still hold on to same people as friends? Maybe we should first talk about who a friend is.

A friend is a person with whom you have a bond or mutual affection and closeness, one typically exclusive of sexual or family relations. Your friend loves you, respects you, and trusts you. They readily accept you for who you truly are, defend you, and also look you in the face to tell you the truth — sweet or bitter.

In recent times, we have increasingly seen friends, and the resultant concept of peer pressure, become the reason for very bad actions and terrible behavioral changes. From entering an unhealthy relationship to taking drugs, to getting hooked to pornography, to involvement in gambling and the likes..., just to name a few.

Hey, Friends

It was for this reason I became deliberate with choosing my friends. When I returned to school, I watched out for girls like myself who had purity, Godliness and good character as values. Did I find any? Sure as heaven! And with them, it was easy to handle my emotions going forward. Our conversations were not like the ones I had with the girls in my neighborhood two years earlier. In this new group, boys were not the focus; God, school and our future were. It is not as if we sat down to have a class on being a good girl, it just happened unceremoniously. It was natural, because of what we focused on and filled our minds with.

My new friends took pride in keeping their bodies pure. They were glad and unashamed to be different from others. Unfortunately, what is prevalent today is that many teenagers feel sad, cheated, and sometimes ashamed when standing for purity and living chaste lives, whereas the ones hopping from one bed to another and doing all the wrong things act confidently and boldly. This is an anomaly. We ought to be the light and lead with excellent examples unapologetically.

In my case, before long that sense of pride caught up with me and I began to square my shoulders from knowing that I was chaste. I prided myself in it unashamedly.

Hey, Friends

> When you decide firmly to lead a clean life, chastity
>
> will not be a burden to you,
>
> it will be a crown of triumph.
>
> — St. Josemaria Escriva

In this circle, it was no longer a struggle saying 'no' to advances from guys who kept coming, or reading one book that will leave my mind filthy, or learning the lyrics of a song that didn't edify. It was a total package. I had the power to turn away. And I was happier for it. Purity is Power!

Let me say here that as a teen it is not abnormal to chase or be chased, especially if you find yourself in environments where there are lots of youths. It is not even a function of whether you are handsome, pretty, smart, or rich; it is more of the fact that teenage is puberty age, and puberty comes with hormones generally thought by professionals to increase a teenager's desire for sex. That is why you must get yourself armed with knowledge and skills, as well as the right friendships to help you swim against the tides.

Hey, Friends

In choosing and making friends, especially as a teenager, one common phrase that comes to play almost every time is Peer Pressure.

Peer Pressure refers to the influence that people of the same age or social group can have on each other. Although peer pressure does not necessarily have to be negative, the term "pressure" implies that the process persuades them to do things that they may be resistant or reluctant, or not chosen to do.

For example, peer pressure is used when people are talking about behaviors that are not considered socially acceptable or desirable, such as experimentation with sex, alcohol, drugs, truancy, etc. Or have you heard the term typically being used to describe socially desirable behaviors like exercising or studying?

Peer Influence

Is the capacity to have an effect on the character, development, or behavior of someone or something, or the effect itself. It is when a young person encourages another to get involved in certain activity — usually beneficial. This includes leading them to exposure to a Godly, healthy lifestyle, appropriate role models,

Hey, Friends

intentional decision-making, and ultimately leading them to become positive role models themselves.

So, if you must have a healthy sexuality, you must deliberately seek for Peer Influencers, not Peer Pressurizers.

Some wise sayings:

It's better to be alone than be with the wrong friends.

A wise person learns from their mistakes, but a wiser person learns from others' mistakes.

Show me your friends and I will tell you who you are.

Who you follow determines what follows you.

One of the wisest decisions you will make is the friends you choose.

Choose your friends; don't let them choose you.

Friendship is not by force; it is by choice.

I heard of a girl who was sincerely a good girl. Not like her friends at all, but she kept them anyway, with the thought that she could handle whatever pressure they brought her way. Soon she had a boy ask her out, and she refused. After much pestering, he decided to go.

Hey, Friends

through her friends. Trust bad girls to love all the attention young rich kids come with (parents' car, money, recharge cards, gifts, snacks, and all the stuff any youth would like). His mission was to get her friends on his side so they could help him on this project. And help him they did, because before long they had succeeded in persuading their friend to accept. You can guess how it ended. Such relationships are usually no good.

In an only boys' school in one of the big cities in Nigeria, a story was told at my bi-monthly teens club several years ago. A certain city "big boy" had the habit of coming to befriend two or three boys in SS3 (Senior Secondary 3) class. His style was to bring the latest iPhone just released. When he succeeded, he would begin to have sexual relations with them. And so this particular set was already aware and were prepared not to give in. But when teenagers have not mastered the art of contentment, they fall into the traps of such evil men. The man got a victim, who would rather have the latest iPhone than keep his purity (yes, boys can and should have a healthy sexuality too). He received the phone and the attention that came with it, and of course pressured his friend to join him. Later, those boys began to have lots of issues with their academics, physical health and mental state.

Hey, Friends

Your friends surround you like a fence, so ensure you fortify yourself by choosing wise friends. Some friends just derive pleasure in getting you to do the wrong things that they are doing. It's a guilt-trip mechanism. So, they can go to any length, even if it means betraying you, just to get you to fall.

Proverbs thirteen: twenty,

> Walk with the wise and become wise; associate with fools and get in trouble.

A fool is a person who acts unwisely or imprudently; a silly person, who tricks or deceives someone.

The way to choose your friends is to acknowledge what your values are. It's a skill you must learn and use. You choose friends based on your own values. What do you cherish? What are the things of worth to you? What are you most unwilling to give up? What are the risks you can't afford to take? You cannot value purity and your friends value pornography. You cannot value integrity and your friends value outsmarting others. No way! Your values must align or be ready to fall with time.

Hey, Friends

Daniel and his friends, in Daniel one: eleven to fifteen, decided not to defile themselves with food sacrificed to idols. They didn't have one of them going behind their back to get supplies from the palace. They decided and stood by their decision, because it was what they all wanted.

It's time to profile or audit your friends. Drop some and add some, so you don't run into trouble.

But to start, the greatest friend you need is Jesus. With Him in your life you are guaranteed of a life without crushing crises — relationship, health, mental, physical, and any other form of crisis.

Please say this prayer right now — and mean it: Lord Jesus, I come to you today as a sinner who has wronged You in every way. I ask that you forgive me of all my sins and wrongdoings. Today, I receive you into my life as personal Lord and Savior and I ask that you will come into my heart and cleanse me with your blood. Be that friend that sticks closer than a brother, and at the end of time may I meet You face to face, in Your beauty and glory, in Jesus name I have prayed.

The journey continues...

CHAPTER three
WHO IS IN THE GARDEN?

Have you heard the children play rhyme: "Who is in the garden? A little fine girl. Can I come and see her? No, no, no, no!..."

We sang that rhyme throughout primary school, with a group of children in a circle and their hands locked-in tightly to each other. The song usually ends with a question as someone goes around the circle (from outside) and tries to break through. He asks, "Can I pass?", and we answer "No way!" He keeps trying until he is able to break through by cutting loose two hands.

A wise man once said a group is as strong as the weakest person in it. I want to ask you, "Who is in your garden?" Your garden here represents your association, your environment. This is bigger than the group of friends you keep. A garden hosts various groups of people, so it's a bigger circle. An association is a group of people organized for a joint purpose. For a teenager, this could mean a teen's club, a mentoring club, a sports group, etc. It also extends to a school, fellowship, teens church, etc. The key thing is that they have a common purpose.

Who is in the Garden?

Recently, one of my male mentees shared with us how in his secondary school the rate of immorality is about 98%. It is so bad that students would sleep with each other in broad daylight. A messy sight, he recalled.

When he attempted to revive the chapel that was now being used as one of their hangouts, he was threatened, insulted and mocked. He didn't find up to two people to join him in that fight. It was a really tough time for him.

I perfectly understood his plight because I would have been really frustrated if I didn't have a place to fellowship frequently, in my own secondary school days too. The Fellowship of Christian Students (FCS) was our place of growth. Bible Study and Sunday services were soul-lifting. It was as if every time you got in there, the Holy Spirit replaced the desire for the opposite sex with a deep longing for God Himself.

When it was time to leave school, it was a very difficult time for me. I was scared of what would happen in this 'wild world', as our patrons and advisors called it then. It was like my cover was taken off, my safe place, my haven, my comfort zone. But we had to move. And that's life; change must happen.

Who is in the Garden?

Of course, the transition was not easy, but the word stuffed in my spirit sustained me for many months. I have hidden your word in my heart that I might not sin against you (Psalms one hundred and nineteen: eleven).

It seemed there was an unleashing of young boys — good, bad and handsome alike. Many of them were on the lookout for freshers like us. So, it was a 'No' galore. I woke up every morning thinking of the number of guys I had to say "no, I can't", "no, I won't" to in the politest manner. Yes, let me add that, as a teenage girl (and boy of course), you must learn to have refusal skills if you must stay sane in this sexualized world where everyone wants to ask you out. We'll discuss that later. (Temptations will always come, but temptation needs your cooperation!)

I had this deep hunger for a gathering, an association of youths that shared my values. You are lucky that these days almost every church has a teens church. In my day, we didn't have that opportunity. There were children's church and the adult church, while teens were left out, so they seized the opportunity to socialize.

Because the law of attraction works anywhere, you will attract what you desire. I suddenly heard of a youth fellowship known as FECA (Federal Ex-students Christian Association). God bless the visionary. FECA was a life saver. In fact, I can't stress that enough. It was a proper definition of people in a group with a common goal, which was to grow spiritually. Know this: "When you stop learning, you stop growing; and when you stop growing, you start dying."

The word of God in FECA was second to none. In retrospect, that was the word that sustained many of us throughout our days in the university. Our leaders then made it a point of duty to listen to our fathers in the faith like Bishop David Oyedepo, Pastor E.A. Adeboye, Pastor Paul Adefarasin, Pastor David Ogbueli, and other ministers who had God's word for youths. They would listen and break it down to our level. We loved the Word. It was majorly centered on revival, evangelism and righteousness. The title of this book, Maintain Your White, was the title of a message preached by one of us back then — Brother Efa Arikpo. This is 20 years after I heard that message and it has not left my mind. The topic stood out for me because it was like an instruction, a warning, a counsel, and an impartation. I still hear it in my spirit till now. It was my motto!!!

FECA had the value of purity. All through my stay in the

university, I never heard of any scandal involving a member or leader. You might doubt it, but it's the truth. And it's not because we prayed so much; it was because the culture of accountability partners was very strong. We understood as youths that our emotions were raging, so we watched each other's back. We gave each other permission to query our relationships. We engaged in activities after lectures. So, it was either you are in school or you are having meetings, then back to school to read at night. We moved in clusters. In the hostel, we stayed in groups. We paid each other surprise visits. Honestly, you couldn't tell which brother or sister would come knocking on your door at any time of the day or night.

In FECA, you didn't have any choice but to grow spiritually. Peer influence (not pressure) was tangible. You could see your peers striving to please Jesus and you would just love it and follow suit. FECA was my first encounter with Peer Mentoring. It was not a boring place. There, you would meet sweet-spirited, bubbly, lively, and funny people. Such an awesome phase of my life.

Our parents were aware of us. Our classmates and friends all knew we were FECA-ites and we stood for purity. We couldn't *fall our hand* and disappoint all these people who looked up to us.

FECA was a place of revival, a powerful vision really needed at that time. It was a bridge between secondary school and university. The Association truly understood the struggles we were having as youths at that time.

I remember the story of Lot in the Bible, a very interesting read from Genesis nineteen: four to eight. Lot lived and associated with evil men, and when he had male visitors, a mob came against him to rape his guests. Lot begged so hard that he even offered his daughters to the men, but to no avail. Question is, why did Lot continue to live there? He lived in a place where his association was deeply rooted in so much evil that it eventually affected both him and his daughters' decisions.

Offering his virgin daughters to the evil men was very wrong. And later we see that his daughters got him drunk and raped him. Bible scholars query Lot's actions as being hypocritical and ungodly in nature. Like them, I also wonder why he was living in Sodom in the first place? Why did he choose to go there? It is probably true that Lot was a God-fearing man to some extent, but he obviously was compromising his values and was probably being influenced by the sinfulness of the city. In his compromised position, he sinned by offering his daughters. The lesson for us here is that even if we are righteous, associating with ungodly people can influence us directly and/or indirectly.

I hear teenagers complain: "church is boring", "school fellowship is boring", "your group of Godly friends are not dope", "your teammates who talk about things that will benefit you are far from 'fresh'". I wonder if you can really survive in a 'fresh' but sexually active group without giving in. You should change your perspective and begin to look at things in a whole new way. Appreciate a genuine Godly environment; it's an asset of inestimable value.

If you are in dire need, like some of the teenagers who come to the Teens Roundtable, for a group of people to stir you up to grow spiritually, you will find one. I once heard Apostle Joshua Selman say "Your environment has a way of responding to what is inside of you." So, do not be discouraged. You will find what you seek.

However, sometimes it might be a call for you to begin the revival, while others join you later.

Who is in the Garden?

If you are in a gathering that stirs up that bad side of you, you need to take a walk out of that garden. Some are in cult groups, social groups that want you to do what God displeases. Take a leave now before they destroy you!

I want to sound a note of warning at this point that you must be alert in any association you find yourself, so that if by chance the values the group upholds begin to change, if certain behaviors are now creeping in, then that's another time to either cry for help or take a walk. Never ever beat your chest and say you can withstand whatever happens. The Bible says, "Let he that thinks he stands take heed lest he falls".

A few months back, one of my teens in church told me he and a group of his school mates decided to start a school fellowship since there was none, and I counseled him on what to do. One of most importance was to ensure that they had teachers supervising them and serving as pastor leaders, because although teens feel they can handle whatever comes their way as they seek independence, what they actually need is guided independence. It wasn't up to two months and he came running back to complain that the student choir mistress was being distracted by a certain boy who wouldn't let her be. He looked at me and said, "Aunty, you were right."

Who is in the Garden?

My counsel was simple. "Do all you can to restore her. She needs Godly girls who can help her through this period, and she needs a teacher to mentor her." Then I ended with this: "If you don't nip it in the bud now, that same attitude will go around, because the spirit of unrighteousness will hover around. That's how certain attitudes enter a group from one to another."

As teenagers, you sometimes don't have much choice when it comes to the school you go and where you live, because those are decisions fundamentally taken by your parents. But I believe that with this knowledge you are gaining, you can have a word with your parents, calling their attention to the ungodliness and immorality that prevail in a place where you are. It's actually a good reason to leave the place.

You must understand that teen-age is a good time to build yourself up for the great and colorful future ahead of you. It's a time to sow seeds of righteousness, so go ahead and do so.

This is not saying that you should become a recluse, that is, a person who lives a solitary life and tends to avoid other people. You cannot be a lonely loner. In fact, that is risky, because when you are out of a circle you can be attacked by depression, become addicted, suffer low self-esteem issues, etc.

I heard of some girls in a secondary school who were reading their books during a social night where other girls were presenting comedy, drama and choreography under the supervision of their teachers. No! You are free to socialize with your peers, but to do so responsibly. You must know where to cross the line, and if you make a mistake, be free to go back to God. We also made mistakes then, and you will too. This is not a call to perfection, but a call to a determination to keep going on this purity journey and making decisions to make the journey worthwhile.

Let's go there...

CHAPTER four
WHERE DO YOU HANGOUT?

As a teen, it is not abnormal to feel restless, bored, or even idle sometimes. You get tired of routines easily and always crave something new. The level and intensity of restlessness varies amongst teens, depending mostly on their personalities. Some are more agile than others, while some are introverts and would rather stay indoors. But whatever the case, teens need a spark in their lives.

Adolescence is also a stage of exploration, so teenagers are constantly testing their ability to take the right decisions on where to go and not to go, and what to do or not do. In school, we heard of youths who would leave their campuses and go to other campuses in other states. Wow, such risk! They would go for parties, night shows, long visits and all sorts, mostly without their parents or guardians' knowledge or consent.

This was the case of Dinah (Jacob's only daughter) in Genesis thirty-four: one and two.

Leah's daughter Dinah, whom Leah bore to Jacob, went out to see some of the young women of the area. She was seen by Hamor's son Shechem, the leader of the Hivites, and he grabbed her and raped her.

Where Do You Hangout?

Boredom, clueless movements and an unbridled decision to move without first considering her environment led to that mishap.

Many times when I have opportunity to speak with such teens, they often say they want to be left alone to enjoy their lives. I understand that feeling because Teens are generally very curious. Do you feel the same way? Do you feel you need to explore the entire universe and catch all the fun the world has to offer? Not a bad idea at all, if you ask me; but to what end, I would ask you.

I want you to know that scientists say that the part of the teenage brain responsible for making critical decisions is not fully developed and won't be until in their twenties. Therefore, teens are more likely to make wrong decisions, especially when they are left unguided. That explains why a teenager can have exams just ahead, but will throw caution to the wind, miss his lectures and paint the whole town red, partying. I think it's worse now because we have teenagers going into tertiary institutions at a younger age than was the norm some years ago.

Having said that, I need you to know that you can be

Where Do You Hangout?

deliberate about how you channel your energy and where you take your feet to. For me, it was a time to attend conferences, seminars, camps, workshops, theater dramas, plays and comedy shows.

Many of the conferences and seminars I attended were for youths and singles. I particularly loved those because the fact that we were abstaining from sexual indulgence didn't mean we were exempted from dreaming. As a matter of fact, the conferences helped me to catch a picture of what I wanted my marriage and future husband to be, and that helped me to stay focused on the real deal. Remember, what you focus on soon becomes your reality.

What these programs did for me was build my capacity, teach me new skills, sharpen old ones and encourage me to keep going on the journey. It was in those programs I learnt the real consequences of having sex before marriage. I learnt that there was more to fornication than just getting pregnant.

At those conferences and seminars, we were taught the right and proper perspectives to sex. We were taught abstinence, developing a pure heart, healthy sexuality, etc.

Where Do You Hangout?

Again, sexual purity doesn't come by chance; it comes by deliberate programming. I see purity like a career that you choose, plan towards and work for. And to do that you must be mindful of where you take your feet to.

These programs were the opportunity we had to start listening to recorded messages on CDs, etc. Remember, what you listen to determines what you think. So, I am an advocate for listening to motivational and inspirational speeches, rather than listening to unhealthy music that leaves you feeling sensational and puts you in a sex mood. Being one who works with teens, I know that teens can have their earpiece on for hours, so why don't you use that time to invest into your spirit things that are beneficial and will profit you both now and in the future?

Maybe you're saying to yourself: 'but I'd rather read a book or work on my computer, write articles, etc.' all day long. That is fine. But, trust me, social connection is very important to your wholesome development as a teen or youth. You sometimes need to let down your hair, relax and exhale. You need balance. These programs I talk about are one of such ways to do so in a Godly manner.

Where Do You Hangout?

When such programs are organized, much effort goes into adding a lot of spice to them. Like comedy, music, spoken word, etc. It's always such a sweet time in God's presence, learning new things in an amusing and unforgettable manner. Such events are void of inappropriate behavior, vocal foul language and swear words.

These days we have summer camps, vacation camps, etc. I host one yearly called the Teens Mentoring Boot camp. I literally always feel the excitement in the teens as they gather for a few days to be mentored on life, leadership and entrepreneurial skills. It is in such camps I see teens discover themselves, find purpose, begin the process to build healthy self-esteem and Godly character.

Today, I see teens and young adults (some already in their early 20s) who have never attended any camp meeting or youth conference. I want to encourage you to begin to attend.

This journey of sexual purity is not an easy one, I must say, and it can never be a success without a solid support system. Do not forsake the gathering of believers, because God commands His blessings there and avails grace to live above sin.

Where Do You Hangout?

Please stop the "lonely Londoner" lifestyle already. Get in the midst of trustworthy people who share the same values as yourself. It doesn't have to be a fellowship like mine. It could be a teens club, a social club, a school club, but by all means don't be outside a positive circle. My mentor, Pastor Mrs. Opi Agha would say: "When the devil wants to hit you, he will take you out of the circle, then strike." Don't ever believe everyone is corrupt. No way! I believe there's a remnant of God's people with whom you can fellowship.

I wish you know how some adults envy you for having such beautiful experiences that will help you shape your destiny ahead. Enjoy it while it lasts.

However, be alert when you go to such places, as when you go to any other gathering. Be careful who you hang around. Some youths come to such events to pass time and distract others. They make noise, refuse to participate, giggle while using their phones, pass notes, etc., especially when an important information is being passed or activity is going on. At any point at those events, you can catch a vision for your life, get an idea that can change your world or even hear a word that will change your life forever.

CHAPTER five

LOOK INSIDE YOUR HEAD

Many times, when you hear two people arguing or engaging in a fight, you hear the question "Do you know who I am?", and that tends to focus on their strength, physical looks, and maybe financial/social status. I think people should shift attention from who they are to what they know. Because you are a product and sum total of what you know.

When the Bible said "...in all your getting (and acquisition), get understanding", it was placing the value of knowledge above everything else. As a youth, understanding would be your greatest asset. And one way to get it is by acquiring knowledge.

The first and major reason anyone has sex before marriage is a lack of understanding. I will explain this more explicitly later.

A popular saying asserts that experience is the best teacher; but do you know that the cost of learning from your own mistakes is very expensive and sometimes unaffordable? Funny, but true. A wise man said, "Wise

Look Inside Your Head

people learn from their mistakes, but wiser people learn from others' mistakes."

This should be the attitude of teenagers and young adults. "Buy the truth and sell it not", because life is a personal race. Go for knowledge, so you can use your head to stay ahead. When you know what to do and what not to do in any situation, you can never be caught unawares in the sex web.

Now, how can you acquire the knowledge to help you live a sexually pure life? Primarily by reading relevant books. If you like reading, I am sure you probably had a smile on from reading the last sentence; but if you don't, I perceive you frowned slightly. Can I tell you that you cannot live above or better than what you know? Whether it concerns changing your mindset, building up your character, making decisions, working hard, growing spiritually, or working on your sexuality.

Knowledge, they say, is power. That means knowledge gives you the power to make wise choices, overcome your weaknesses and whatever hinders you from moving forward.

Look Inside Your Head

As an example, if you are about to have sex with someone and, just before the act, you suddenly realize the person has a horrible skin disease that can be contracted by contact, would you proceed? What will likely happen is that your brain will instantly send a message to all parts of your body, especially those directly involved in the act, to say "Stand still; attention!" Correct?

No amount of love profession, promise, or sexual weakness will make you go on with the act. Even those who say they can't control themselves will suddenly find that they are able to. Why? Knowledge has given you power.

As a girl, do you know when a guy likes you? You should. Because, for example, the way he looks at you should reveal that. Should you be confused when a guy sends you gifts and romantic messages all in the name of words of encouragement and inspiration? Sometimes, some guys would be acting all nice towards a girl and claiming to want nothing from her. Story for the gods! (rolls eyes!) They know what they want. And you should know too.

Look Inside Your Head

As a guy, are you serious when you claim to not notice a girl seeking for your attention badly by deliberately exposing and flaunting her body for you? Or when she displays an attitude to you, scolding you for not calling or checking up on her? What of girls who want to do chores for you like cook, bake, do your assignments for you, and defend you firmly? She knows what she is doing, or what she wants. However, I'm not saying this is the case every time, but that you must stay alert always!

Knowledge affects even the little, seemingly unimportant things.

You may want to blame your parents, teachers and mentors for not educating you properly, but I want you to know that sexual purity is your decision to make. And as you approach your twenties, you should seek to learn new skills, improve on your talents, build healthy social connections, understand your emotions and urges.

Do you know we are in the knowledge era? Whatever we need is available on the internet and through technology. With just the click of a button, it's in your face. So, what excuse do you really have for staying ignorant?

Look Inside Your Head

I hear people say the internet is the greatest challenge of the 21st Century child. That may be true, but remember that the other side of the coin makes the internet a solution for nearly any issue. From the internet, you can choose to get articles and other contents to either destroy your life or to build it. The choice is yours. Whereas, in our days, we depended solely on what we were taught. And if we weren't, then so be it. But now, you can learn any skill you want to — if you are serious about it. There are tons of tools, charts, plans and materials to make you a better person. As an experiment, you can try it now if you have an internet enabled device. Ask Google to give you tips on building good character, or a chore chart to keep tabs of what to do daily, etc.

This generation is prone to screen and gadgets, hence, authors have also moved with the trends. Most writers now have their books in soft copy — very convenient to read. And many are even available for free download online. But be sure to get only healthy ones.

The books you read shouldn't be restricted to only relationships, dating, sex, etc. Read books that teach you self-awareness, understanding and managing your emotions, and more. I recall that as a teen, my best friend and I read "Why You Act The Way You Do" by Tim LaHaye. That book was a game changer for me. It explained what my strengths and weaknesses were and how to enhance and overcome them respectively. That book made it easy for me to know the kind of man that I would be most compatible with for marriage.

A book is actually a medium of learning without necessarily going to school. It is a medium for a writer to bring you into their world, across oceans and mountains and very long distances. The concept from one book can change your perspective about life forever, and in a few minutes.

Most relationship books are actually very interesting. Nowadays, you don't even have to spend a fortune buying books, because of the electronic media we have available. The internet is a leveler. Both the rich and the poor, the wise and the ignorant all have access to knowledge through the internet.

In my teenage years, we had limited access to information. The internet was not popular, yet it was expensive. Nonetheless, we had access to CDs, tapes, books, and informative magazines. But some teenagers

Look Inside Your Head

would rather spend their time with soft porn magazines because they had pictures that caught their attention and became addictive — sadly. They hid themselves to do this and thought they were being smart; unknown to them, they were doing more harm to themselves than good.

We had to visit cyber cafes to pay for internet browsing time, but today you have access on your mobile phones and tablets. That means you have no excuse to lack quality information.

I remember listening to a teaching on CD many years ago where a preacher explicitly explained how having sex with someone who is not your spouse joins you both in body and soul. So, if your "sin partner", as I choose to call it, has challenges that run through their family, then prepare to get a bit of it in your own life. Let me say here that some of us are auditory learners, while others are visual. But you will need to combine all the learning styles so as not to miss out on vital information.

You will still need knowledge of what to do as you prepare for marriage (when the time approaches), what to look out for in a responsible spouse. Sex is not a teacher, wisdom is; and you get wisdom by reading.

Look Inside Your Head

I laugh when I hear people say they want to date and have sex with their girlfriend/boyfriend to know if they will make good future spouses. Oh my God! That is such a huge lie. There is no way of knowing that way. As a matter of fact, pre-marital sex blinds your eyes to certain key things you should observe in a person. Lots of people tried that and regret it till this day.

As a teen, I learned while reading that I have three gates that are key to my life: my eyes, ears and heart gates, because what I see, hear and think are a direct determinant of how I act and who I eventually become.

If you know and understand this early in life, you will not accept just anything all because your friends say it's cool and the world says it's sexy.

Again, like I said, I see teenagers on their phones for long periods, listening to unedifying music that arouses their emotions and puts them in a sexual mood. Whereas, they should be listening to edifying songs with inspiring lyrics or speeches from motivational speakers that can spark off buried talents in them, or unutilized strengths.

Look Inside Your Head

Look, everyone was born with a solution for at least one of life's problems. You don't have to be perfect to fulfill purpose; you only need to realize what your purpose is, accept it, and pursue it.

There is no vacuum in life. If you are not pursuing purpose and focused on your vision, then anything passing by is permitted to fill up that void in your life. That includes partying, clubbing and just chilling (a.k.a. wasting your time – sorry, your life). Remember, an idle mind is the devil's workshop.

I must warn that you must be disciplined when getting knowledge on the internet. For example, you were going to learn something on YouTube when suddenly you saw a headline pop-up on your screen: "Pick the hottest date here" or "what to do to get the best boyfriend in town", followed by "click to watch". Ignorantly, you click and it leads you to pornographic sites. That is the end of your online training and the beginning of your journey to addiction. God forbid!

As you seek for knowledge, be deliberate about building your character and discipline. Resist every form and appearance of evil. Focus on what's important – your

Look Inside Your Head

growth and sexual purity. The level of purity you exhibit is directly linked to the level of knowledge you have. For example, I have heard people say you can be a virgin — avoid sexual intercourse — and yet indulge in other acts like kissing, smooching, etc. That is both foolish and untrue. Why do you want to awaken a sleeping viper? Why awaken love when it is not time? This is why knowledge is so critical!

Are you feeling like Purity is hard work? (LOL) I actually understand that feeling, but trust me, like every other thing in life that we labour for, you will soon discover that there is much profit in Purity. Don't quit.

CHAPTER six
I GOT MY MIND MADE UP

The mind is where the will of man resides. It is where thinking happens. Every physical outcome of your life first happened in your mind. This is why people say sex is in the mind. Your mind first creates a picture, then your body follows. The mind births vision. The mind is a gift from God and a valuable asset. When things go wrong, stop the blame game and check your mindset.

The fact is, after you change your friends, get planted in the right circle and association, go to the right place of worship, listen to quality teachings, read books, attend conferences and seminars, and even do more than I have taught in this book. If you do not make up your mind and make a personal vow to yourself to stand for sexual purity, somewhere along the line you just might fall by the wayside.

Personal vows, commitments and resolutions are so powerful that not even Satan and his agents, or the whole of hell, can make you do what you have purposed to not do. Interestingly, even God cannot stop you or make you do

I Got My Mind Made Up

what you don't want to do. He gave us the power of choice and cannot take it away from us. He gives you options, advises you on which to choose, and allows you heed or reject the counsel. If it were not so, then David, who was God's anointed lover, wouldn't have slept with Bathsheba. God called David a man after His heart, but he was overcome by lust and a lack of inward strength to fight back the temptation he faced. As a result, he fell.

Again, God has given man a precious, powerful, and irrevocable gift. And that gift is the power of choice. Everything that happens in life is by human choices.

When it comes to personal vows, we should stand for righteousness. Can you guess who that worked for in the Bible? Joseph! For your information, Joseph was a teenager when Potiphar's wife was pressuring him to go to bed with her. He was also at a downtime in his life because he had been sold by his brothers to a strange land. Someone who was very attached to his father had been sold as a slave. In Nigeria, we call a child, like Joseph an *"ajebutter"*, that is, a pampered child. Now, because of his brothers' envy, he became a slave house-boy.

Joseph could have given himself that as an excuse, but he didn't – because he chose not to. Joseph, in Genesis thirty-nine: nine(b) said, "How could I do such a wicked thing? It would be a great sin against God." He called premarital sex 'wickedness against God!' Wow! What wisdom he had at an early age! Oh, how can your creatures, the works of Your hands do wickedness ever so often and feel no remorse or need for repentance? Have mercy, Lord!

After I graduated from secondary school and awaited my O'level (GCE) results, I got admitted into a Polytechnic. To keep me from getting bored at home, I took the admission and started ND 1, pending when my result would be out. But there was a condition that if my result came and I didn't pass Mathematics, I'll step down to the lower class (Preliminary class), then also known as "Senior SS3 class". But I hoped I wouldn't. So, I started my ND with faith in my heart. I settled-in nicely and made new friends. Soon, I met this young man who was dark, of average height, but extremely handsome. He loved me so (isn't that what we always think, ladies?). A

I Got My Mind Made Up

guy looks at you admiringly, shows care and concern for you, then you believe he is really going to die for you. Funny! Anyway, I also liked him very much. And this can happen the other way around. I recently heard of a young girl who showered a guy so much love and attention the boy wanted to run away. (LOL) Oh yes, some girls could be that desperate!

Anyway, he said he loved me and never failed to state the fact that I was smart, from a good home, and very well-behaved. But, with all the care and attention, I knew deep in my heart that dating was a no-go area for me. Because it all starts from chatting, hugging, then kissing, touching, and eventually sex. So, I didn't even want to start.

I made sure I was always with my female friends so that whether he was visiting or vice versa, I was never alone. But on this fateful day, it was announced that our long awaited GCE results were out. It was a defining day for me. A Credit in Mathematics meant ND would continue for me, but a Pass meant stepping down to preliminary class – after all the posing as a Year One student. So, I

I Got My Mind Made Up

eagerly and anxiously went to check, and my fears happened – I didn't make a Credit. I came back to school beaten, battered, and shattered. My world seemed to be crashing. How can I, I asked myself, who just finished from the prestigious Airforce Girls Military School, Jos, Plateau State, where only two students were picked per state every year, now "fall so hard"? Those days, Airforce Girls were treated like the nation's babies – so much prestige and honor. All that, was going to be lost in the twinkle of an eye. I was falling from my high horse. I asked God questions for what I did to deserve this. I told Him how some of my mates were already in universities. I whined, complained, nagged. My faith shook that day. I felt like giving up on this God whom I felt had let me down. That was my mood when I first got back to school that day.

Guess who I met as I got into school? Yes, him! See temptation! He immediately noticed my sad countenance and tried to comfort and console me. Tears streamed down my eyes and no amount of jokes could make me smile or cheer up. So he quickly suggested we

I Got My Mind Made Up

go to his house. Of course, I agreed; I had no strength to even argue. I just nodded and followed him. You won't believe that for the first time ever, my friend was not in school (see set up!). I was left alone to my fate.

There actually comes a day when you will be faced with temptation. The Bible calls it the day of adversity; where your stand for purity will be tested. Oh, I would never forget that day! We got to his house alongside two of his friends. We had conversations, refreshments, etc. Then the moment came. All of a sudden, his friends stood up and left the room, smiling stylishly and sheepishly. I was left alone with him. My heart began to beat as he came close to me. "Ghen Ghen!" So this is it? Then my brain suddenly woke up. My emotions told me: "Relax. Remember you're sad, depressed and disappointed. Remember you need this. Just relax..." But my mind shouted: "No! This was not the plan. You need to stop this, and you need to stop it now!". As he came closer, I turned my face away. That was one of the hardest things to do in that instant, I must confess. But I remembered my vow, I remembered the picture of my future.

I Got My Mind Made Up

I remembered I was to stay sexually pure until I got married. Pictures of me getting married to my husband chaste came to my mind quickly. I remembered I had the power to stand up and get out. I mean, I was not going to get raped; so if I did this, I chose to, not forced. I remembered all the times my friends and I had conversed and it seemed like we had planned and prepared for this day by affirming and reaffirming our purity vow.

My dear, that moment came; the turning point where I *"borrowed myself some sense."* As he started speaking English, "You know I love you... blah, blah, blah..." I stood up, wore my shoes and took off like a cheetah. Not even a kiss, not even a peck. I don't know how I did it that day, but I believe the power of choice and a personal vow for purity is the best thing that can happen to any teenager. I ran off like Joseph did. Thankfully, he didn't come after me. I guess he was in shock of how I could wriggle out of that well-set situation. Or maybe he was disappointed with himself for not being able to pull off this one. Whatever the case was, thanks to God and the voice of reason from my spirit.

I Got My Mind Made Up

My dear teenager, when you come so close to having sex with someone who is not your spouse, it is your inner voice (voice of the Holy Spirit in you) that will give you strength to take off. As I always say to my mentees, when you're in such a scene, you don't pray, watch or speak – you take off, run, flee. As fast and far as you can! Use your feet, not your mouth!

It is that voice that will give you a sense of reason and energize your feet for flight. But that voice will only amplify what has been said already. So, it is very important what you say to yourself daily. At the moment of temptation, that will be your life saver.

Don't let a deliberately crafted sex-stimulating world take your senses. And even if it does, get some sense and disallow its deceit. Needless to say, I earned that young man's respect that day. The next time he saw me, he gave me a look as if to say "this girl, you're strong." Whatever it was, I was free – and proud of it. I had made my point and had kept my bed undefiled.

Joseph, the one who moved from prison to the palace – by the way, that is one prophetic declaration that makes church

I Got My Mind Made Up

folks scream a resounding "Amen!" – but do we even know how Joseph got to prison? He got there because of a personal vow to not sin against God and defile himself. His master's wife framed him, but Joseph was ready to go to jail and suffer rather than sin against God.

Do you know that if he had laid with his master's wife, he may have received more salary, more favor, and maybe less work at home? But he chose not to. This is proof that all the excuses we give because we can't make a vow and stand by it are lame. Instead we blame others, our circumstances, the nation, etc. This scenario is common today. Teachers and lecturers put girls under so much pressure for sex. The girls say it is exchange for good grades. The rich lady tells the young man she will take care of his bills. The "sugar daddies" (or "small gods" as they're now called in Nigeria) will ensure you have all the good things of life as a girl. In other settings, the employer insists you'd remain in their company only if you have sex with them. Guys tell other guys that they're not a man yet, like them, until they sleep with a virgin girl. Terrible world we live in!

Maybe you've lost your parents and things are tight financially. Yes, you practically have every reason to fornicate for money, but I want you to remember this: a personal decision must stem from the fact that you cannot do such wickedness against the Lord your God! So, no amount of peer pressure, threat of failure, lack and want, or mockery from friends should compel or make you defile yourself. Be willing to give up anything for purity sake – fame, friends, fortune. Never put any achievement in life above pleasing God; it's really not worth it.

Don't stop! We are still on this journey...

CHAPTER seven
YOU THINK YOU'VE GOT TALENT?

We are in the days of passion business. Emphasis has gradually shifted from paid jobs to business. Lucky you, dear teen; you've got a chance to be productive (and profitable, of course).

Productivity is the quality, state, or fact of being able to generate, create, enhance, or bring forth goods and services. In most nations of the world, teenagers are not expected to do a proper job until they are 18 years old, but there is no age restriction to doing the business of your talent or turning a passion into business. Mind you, there is a gift inside of you. No one is talentless. Everyone has at least one talent. Some have more.

Maximizing your gift is really key for your teenage years, because doing what you love for a fee brings you joy and fulfillment and empowers you financially to overcome the many temptations from a dirty society.

A married man was pestering this young girl – 19 years old – to go out with him but she wouldn't bulge, and in a bid to convince her, he said, "I really want to take you to the

You Think You've Got Talent?

newest Shawarma joint in town." She replied confidently, "I actually make pastries, so there is nothing special about eating it. And even if I feel like having it, I can afford to buy it myself." That was the end of that shameless chase.

You think she was proud and pompous? I think she is a smart and focused girl who knows what she wants for her life and would not exchange her precious body for a cheap pack of pizza or a cup of ice cream.

Many times, I have noticed both girls and boys give in to sexual lures because of "chicken change" and so-called enjoyment. Listen to me: that thing getting you excited can be produced or acquired by yourself!

Teenagers are at a stage of their lives where they can download divine ideas. They are so creative and can do a lot for themselves, especially with the energy they have as an added advantage. But the question is, are you maximizing yours?

The good thing about being productive and profitable is that it naturally helps to put your emotions in check. I always encourage the teens in my circle to start their

You Think You've Got Talent?

own micro and small businesses. In fact, two of my mentees run a small-scale perfume outfit. One makes pretty bags and recently added shoes to match. Another makes hair bows. One other makes Ankara accessories, and so on. When their peers are partying, they are thinking of new fragrances to launch, new customers to connect with and more grounds to cover for more profit. How cool is that?

It's easier to start a business in this century because all the information and the customers to buy are all online. If you choose not to buy and sell products, you can enhance your speaking and writing skills. Even children are launching books, setting up blog sites, etc. It's a world of limitless opportunities right now.

Few years ago, one of my mentees who was always very shy suddenly started to do performances in church. I was shocked. Really shocked. So I asked what changed and she said she learned the art of spoken words on the internet. Several times after service when teens were catching up, she would be rushing home to rehearse for her next performance.

You Think You've Got Talent?

Gradually, she became a bold and confident girl and recently sent me a message to say she is getting invitations to do performances in and out of school, and she has earned the admiration of her friends and family. You can't imagine how happy that made me!

Having a business or being productive earns you the respect of any guy coming after you. Sometimes, it sends a subtle message of "I am busy. Can you get yourself together and do something meaningful with your life?", even before they come too close.

I strongly believe that productivity makes the purity journey smoother and easier. So, get your productivity gears on a high.

CHAPTER eight

WATCH YOUR BACK

As youths, there are things that are common to your age group, but you need to be very careful because they are sinkers; a little of them, and you are going down the drain – right down to self-destruction.

I remember a true-life story of one of my mentees (she has permitted me to share this story with you). At 13, she entered into a relationship with a 25 years old young man (Please don't scream!). In less than a year, the young man took ill and died before she even discovered she was pregnant (Yes, these days we hear of 11 and 12-year-olds getting pregnant, and it's sickening!). Because of lack of care, she lost the pregnancy. But that was the beginning of her woes. She entered into a state of depression and found herself in a wrong circle of guys who introduced her to alcohol and drugs.

She became a truant in school because they spent the time for classes at an undisclosed place drinking and messing themselves up. She went on like that until, like the prodigal son, one day she came to herself (power of the mind!) and told herself she couldn't continue living so carelessly. Her turn around began, and today God has helped her to become a better person on her way to fulfilling destiny. Praise to God!

Yes, she has been forgiven; but a part of her life has an ugly side which she can't erase. I don't want you to go through such path; but if you have, I want you to watch your back and turn around. There is Grace to live right, but you have to want it and go for it.

The following are some of the things you should be careful and guard against; they are like playing with fire.

DATING

The dictionary defines dating as 'go out with someone (boyfriend/girlfriend) in whom one is romantically or sexually interested'. And, your girlfriend is not only a girl who is your friend, as we have been programmed to think. The first meaning in the dictionary of a girl/boyfriend is a person's regular female/male companion with whom they have a romantic or sexual relationship. Check it.

Sadly, the concept of dating has become a trend in this generation. Everyone wants to "date", not understanding what it means and what would be required of you when you date someone. You want to

Watch Your Back

show off your boyfriend/girlfriend to others. You don't want to feel left out, so you "date". Please note that dating is not a need, it is an option you choose.

Dating could be fun and interesting, sincerely, but it is tasking. Dating is hard work. It is distractive. You have to keep up with your partner via calls, texts, chats, hangouts, gifts, etc. When you don't, the person gets upset while you keep apologizing or begging. And when you are unable to meet up, the person dumps you and moves on to the next available person, and you are left with a heartbreak. I also hear teens, when trying to defend themselves, say they are dating people who are not asking for sex. Unfortunately, that may be true now but, trust me, it won't be for long. Because dating without sex soon becomes a BORING relationship. It is normal to want to explore more. That is why you should be careful to not indulge in it in the first place. Remember my story of my first relationship as a teenager?

Majority of teen moms (teenagers who have babies) didn't get impregnated by strangers, it was done by their boyfriends. Why not learn from their mistakes, instead of saying your case is different, yet you are doing the same thing?

Rather than date, I suggest you seek to build healthy, platonic/non-sexual relationships. Enjoy the company of others because he who seeks sexual purity must burst privacy with the opposite sex.

WILD PARTIES

I remember back in school, we would hear stories of how undergraduates like us went to parties where some ended up being raped, some were found dead with their body parts removed, and other gory tales. Indeed, some of these were caused by rival attacks between different cult groups.

It all begins with the activities and events you choose to attend.

Talking about cultism, many initiations took place at parties seeming to be just birthday parties meant to be harmless, yet they turned out to be a channel for perpetrating all manner of evil.

While the Israelites were camped at Acacia Grove, some of the men began going to wild parties with the local Moabite girls. These girls also invited them to attend the sacrifices to their gods and soon the men were not only attending the feast but were also worshipping the idols.

Watch Your Back

— Numbers twenty-five: one and two

I am not saying you cannot attend parties, but before you go, ask yourself a few questions like:

i. Whose party is it?
ii. What would happen there?
iii. What would be served there?
iv. What are the activities that will take place there? and most importantly
v. Who will be there?

A Psychiatric doctor friend of mine shared an experience with my teen group while mentoring them one time. He once had a patient, a girl who went for a party with her boyfriend, and during the party her drink was drugged. She got high and was acting weird, to the extent that they had to call a doctor to inject her. She had to be camped at a hotel for days because she couldn't go home in that state.

I pity her parents. I can only imagine how worry-sick they would have been over her. It's unfortunate that parties have become so wild, with strong drinks, drugs and rape now being their hallmark. Galatians five: nineteen to twenty-one lists sins that will stop you from inheriting heaven; the party spirit is one of them. Please be careful.

Have you heard of a Holy Ghost party? That is where you get high in God, loaded in your spirit to fulfil purpose and destiny, instead of wasting your life. You should look out for and attend such sometimes.

ALCOHOL

These are drinks people take that get them high and lose control of themselves. When you tell youths not to drink, they will tell you to show them where it is written in the scripture. Well, all I can say is that if you truly are a king, then you will do as King Lemuel's mother advised in Proverbs thirty-one: four, and not give yourself to alcohol.

Alcohol is addictive. You usually want to increase your intake. Until you get to the point when you become tipsy and drunk. And at this point you are vulnerable. To be vulnerable means to be exposed to the possibility of being attacked or harmed, either physically or emotionally.

Indulging yourself with alcohol does not prove anything worthwhile. It does not establish that you are a *"happening"*, "cool" or "fresh" boy or girl, as you may think. Rather, it puts you at risk of falling into the temptation of immorality and being susceptible to harm.

SECULAR CONTENT

Secular music and videos are simply non-religious music or videos. Secular means being separate from religion. Many secular songs are sensational. You listen to the song or watch a music video and your whole body is on fire, your passion level increases to the point you want to do something to let out that feeling.

These days, many music videos are of pornographic nature. The girls are almost naked, the words used are foul, the dance steps are alluring. The challenge with these scenes is that even if you don't have sexual intercourse, those images will play in your mind for a long time.

It is unfortunate that the world is so sexualized now that even public places like hospitals, salons, eateries, parks (where children are found), cable channels and even national TV stations are not exempted. We see vulgar videos everywhere. Sometimes, hours after you have left the place of exposure, the song's rhythm and dance steps still play in your mind.

If your heart is not clean, how then can you be said to have a healthy sexuality. It is time to stop teasing those who are deliberate about what they listen to and watch, and start guarding your heart with all diligence. This is where you must take responsibility for your sexuality.

Some teenagers argue that there is nothing wrong with secular music. My question to them is, to what extent will it help you when you need healing, are in trouble, worried, afraid, etc.? Does it motivate and inspire you to aspire, to dream, and to seek to fulfill your dreams? Please be careful of the songs you listen to and even the authors of those songs, because they usually sing from their own experiences and encounters. Some youths have had lust suddenly come on them uncontrollably after they began to expose themselves to certain music. You might be saying: stop being over spiritual. Well, you probably don't understand how life works yet. Things happen from the spirit to the physical. The spirit realm rules and controls this physical realm, and music is very spiritual and imparts the spirit behind it on its listeners.

DRESSING

How you dress is how you will be addressed. I'm sure you've heard that before. Sometimes, our dressing attracts the opposite sex. Dressing is for covering, not for showing how sexy you are. Stop saying you are pure in heart and saying people shouldn't judge you when your dressing is suggestive. Human beings judge from your looks, because we can't see your heart – only God can.

You cannot dress in a particular way and expect to be addressed in a different way. Dressing reflects your mindset, your thoughts and your self-worth. It reveals whether your sexuality is healthy or sick.

Sometimes, it is the way you dress that sends the message that you don't mind having sex – and I am serious. Then you turn around and complain you are under pressure by the opposite sex. Whose fault is it in the first place?

SLEEPOVERS

This is another new trend. It is a situation where children or teens get to spend the night at another house which is not theirs. It could be the home of other family members like cousins, family friends, or even neighbours.

Sleepovers initially used to be for convenience. Maybe a parent is traveling and drops off the child with someone they know and trust. But with time, it became a social and class thing that children look forward to and even insist on doing. The reason being that during sleepovers, there is a particular level of freedom existing in that house and some parents fail to properly supervise and monitor children and teens that come over.

Sleepovers are a good time to exchange ideas and share new habits with each other, which is why you must be careful. I heard my very close friend complain that her children went to their cousin's house and came back with a report that their cousins consistently watched pornography.

I once heard of a parent who watched the CCTV camera footage and discovered what horrible things her children and their friends were doing at night during sleepovers. So sad!

Dear one, please guard against which friends or family members you exchange sleepovers with. If they have bad habits, cut off and insist with your parents that you don't want to visit them. If your parents insist, feel free to tell them why. The time of sleep is a delicate time where God rains ideas on people; you shouldn't spend yours learning or doing the wrong things.

ROMANTIC NOVELS/TV SERIES

Remember I mentioned before, that I read a lot of romantic novels as a child and many years later I still had those scenes playing in my mind. It can be hard or soft copy (there are a lot of apps and websites for that these days). Recently, a favorite book series for children was discovered to have lots of romantic content in it. I saw it myself, and 'shocked' is an understatement for how I felt. Romantic novels are like the road bumps we meet on our sexual purity journey.

As for TV, you know and agree with me that it is really difficult at present to find programs on TV that don't have love scenes and suggestions. Not even cartoons are exempted. Almost every channel you flip through is showing a kissing scene, discussions on sex, and the sort. I know it looks normal and you just love the programs, but you really need to be careful if you must make it on this your purity journey.

Watch Your Back

Other things to watch your back against are drugs, late night shows, etc. As the others, they will corrode your beautiful future and destiny.

CHAPTER nine

COME TELL ME WHY

A survey I carried out amongst teens on why they have sex showed their answers in this format, with the first being the most reason.

A. Ignorance

Proverbs six: thirty-two says,

> The one who commits adultery (or fornication) lacks sense, understanding, intelligence. He who does so would destroy himself. (Emphasis mine)

Adultery and fornication are similar; they have one thing in common – the act of having sex with someone who you are not married to.

Now, what is that sense you are lacking? It is the fact that what you are doing is destroying yourself. That means you are not aware of what your body was created for and the consequences of misusing your body.

Have you ever heard this statement: "It's my life, and I can do whatever I want with it" or "It's my body and I choose to do what I want in any way I want"? That is so

Come Tell Me Why

far from true, because your body is actually not your own. The owner says in First Corinthians six: thirteen, "...body for the Lord and Lord for the body."

When God made your body, He didn't do it just to occupy space or complete creation. He did it to fulfill His own purpose. This is how it works: our heavenly Father is Spirit but needs to accomplish His will here on earth, so He made you and me to carry out that assignment. Only men (human beings) are permitted to exist and perform anything here on earth, based on God's own ordination. As such, the human body remains the only medium through which God can carry out His agenda.

Philippians two: thirteen says He is working in you to will and to do of His good pleasure.

In primary school this phrase was a part of our lives as we were taught personal hygiene. But, in truth, it is a statement to drive home the point for purity: CLEANLINESS IS NEXT TO GODLINESS. Fornicating (having sex with someone you are NOT married to) is uncleanliness. It is filth, ungodliness, and it drives out the Holy Spirit who uses your body as His home to effect great change on earth.

Come Tell Me Why

Why do you want to chase the owner of your body out from it?

This is one of the greatest battles on earth. The battle of ownership.

I think it's really unfair and irreverent to treat God that way. Your heavenly Father who loves you and created you for His glory, to bring Him pleasure and give you a fulfilling life doesn't deserve to be sent packing. No!

What To Do

a. Go for knowledge on what sex really is and what the consequences of engaging in it prematurely are. Some have been discussed in this book. Read other books written by people with a Godly and biblical perspective.

b. Understand that sex before marriage is putting your future at risk.

c. Don't just be hearer, be a doer. Don't scorn the knowledge you have received, calling it "old school". Believe what the Word of God says and don't scorn it. The world might have changed, but God's Word has not.

d. Be willing to learn, unlearn and relearn. If there

are things you knew before that aren't right, don't delay to drop them and imbibe new and better ones.

B. Peer Pressure

There is a very interesting story in Second Samuel thirteen: one to five. Ammon, a young man and the king's son was lusting after a girl (his half-sister). He didn't know how to get her, but his crafty friend Jonadab comes and tells him how.

You seek to belong among a group of friends because it affirms your self-worth and supports you as you go through the rocky paths toward adulthood. So you seek the support, advice and validation of this group. The joy of the acceptance their friendship brings makes you willing to do anything to remain there, including having sex before marriage.

You look at your friends and admire how they seem to be coping with life's challenges and try to copy them. I see some teens who are somewhat loose and – as we say in Nigeria – have *"tear eye"* walking confidently and cheerfully, while the ones living a chaste life act cowardly and sadly like they are missing out on something, and

Come Tell Me Why

something, and sometimes secretly admiring the other group. This is an evil under the sun; it ought not to be. You know what they are doing is wrong but they seem to be handling it well, so you emulate them anyway. You have missed the shot by a long pole, sweetheart.

What To Do

a. Develop a tough skin by standing firm with the right set of values, even if it makes you less popular.

b. Take responsibility for your actions. One of my wise friends once said, "It is not your fault when people give you bad advice, but it is your fault when you take it."

c. Have a sense of pride in yourself and the decisions you take.

d. Say goodbye to that group that constantly models immoral behavior and exerts pressure on you to follow them.

e. Don't let the pursuit for earning the label of being "cool" rob you of your precious purity. Make your own decisions and stand by them even if it would cost you your "cool" reputation.

f. Bear in mind that the consequence of pre-marital sex is personal.

Come Tell Me Why

C. Mindset

Sexual purity starts in the mind. As a man thinks in his heart, so is he (Proverbs twenty-three: seven).

I realize that most teenagers blatantly refuse to pursue sexual purity because they think and believe it is impossible to achieve.

They hear that these days "everyone is doing it", so they believe they are just being normal.

Celebrities have flaunted their baby-mama and baby-daddy status, and because you admire them a lot, you accept it as the norm in your mind. Well, that everybody is doing it doesn't make it right. Or is your name 'everybody'?

They have heard people ask, "who does purity help?" and they feel there is no gain.

Others believe that they can always fornicate; after all, God will always forgive.

Dear teenager, you must erase those lies you have been told about sex from your mind. For goodness sake, who lied to you that that boy/girl really loves you, which made you give in so cheaply to having sex with him/her.

If they truly love you, they will wait. That is the proof of love you should seek.

Sex is not equal to love. Sex will NOT take away depression, or low self-esteem. Sex is not a way of knowing who to get married to in the future; neither is it a way to prove to your friends that nothing is wrong with you. Those are all lies that you have let become a mindset. Let me ask you: how is sex before marriage love-making, as society likes to code or call it, when God is love and He's not in it?

What To Do
   a. Change your mindset. Press 'reset'.
   b. Create a new picture of you staying sexually pure.
   c. Change the friends and circumstances that helped to build that old mindset.
   d. Be careful who has your ears so as not to re-insert that negative mindset.
   e. Determine to stop taking advantage of God's grace, because even when He forgives you, the devil steals from you.

D. Identity Crisis

This means a period of uncertainty and confusion in which a person's sense of identity becomes insecure. This is common with teenagers. The more confident you are and knowing who you are, the less likely you are to have sex before marriage. Some teens give in to pressures to have sex because they lack self-confidence and are looking for others to validate them. So, if it would come from the person asking for sex, then they don't mind. I heard of a teenager who had sex with a guy on the same day she met him, all because he told her she was so beautiful; and no one had ever told her that before, not even herself. So sad! Please, don't ever stray from God to get closer to someone else. You will corrode your self-identity. And, if no one has ever told you that you are beautiful, handsome, or cute, sweetheart, I am saying it to you right now: you are beautiful, handsome, and perfect the way you are! I may not know you in person, but I know that you are beautiful and perfect because God created you; and everything and person He created is beautiful and perfect! Please believe what God says about you and not anyone else's opinion.

Giving your body just to prove your love for your boy/girlfriend doesn't change anything; the crises is an internal one, not a sexual one.

What To Do

a. Identify your strengths and keep them continually before you.

b. Look at your body, accept and admire what you have. Your height, complexion, size, etc. You are beautiful just the way you are. You don't need anyone's validation. God made you perfect, sweetheart!

c. Take responsibility for building up your self-esteem. No one can do it for you.

d. Say words of affirmation to yourself DAILY such as: I am royalty, I think and act like one; my body belongs to God, so I will handle it with care and dignity, etc.

E. Puberty

During your teen years, hormones can cause you to have strong feelings, including sexual feelings. You may have these feelings for someone of the other gender; that's normal. Thinking about sex or just wanting to hear or read about sex is normal. It is normal to want to be held and touched by others, especially of the opposite sex. Sadly, some teenagers have not learned to pass through puberty but have let puberty pass through them, affecting the quality of their lives.

They experience change in emotions and have not learned how to handle them, so they allow their emotions, how they feel and their moods to determine their sexuality per time.

This is a good time to mention that the teenage years is the time when you hear the word 'crush' a lot. Teens are always crushing on someone. LOL. A crush is a brief feeling of infatuation towards someone. And, as Mrs. Favour Nwaka says in her book *Crush That Crush*, if you don't crush it, it can crush you. That means do not allow it stay longer than it should. Do everything to get that lustful feeling out of your heart because a crush can actually crush you; it can make a mess of you. I have seen teens suspend their brain and take very wrong decisions because they had a crush on someone.

Do you know sex carries great emotional power? That is why a "break up" can cause a "heart break" and "life break". Teenagers generally are unable to combine sex and emotional intimacy. I mean, you are simply too immature for that. You may argue with me now, but you will understand what I mean in a few years' time when you become an adult. But before then, don't take wrong decisions now that you'll regret or be unable to repair.

What To Do

a. Identify your weaknesses and seek to work on them intentionally. Seek help, if you need to from someone mature and respectable near you. Preferably, the person should be of the same gender as you.

b. Have accountability partners that you can truly express how you feel to without being judged. I suggest a senior person, either a teacher, coach or mentor. Either of your parents can also be your accountability partner. Free yourself from guilt by naming and shaming your addictions or secret struggles, and that will best be done to a person who is not your peer.

c. Study yourself and understand your emotions and mood swings. These two sometimes determine our approach to sexual advances per time. See table below for more understanding.

d. Exercise. Play games – outdoor games. Football, gymnastics, basketball, etc. are very beneficial to a teen's health. Games and exercise are a good and positive way of exerting your energy.

Come Tell Me Why

Emotions and Your Sexuality

As a young person, you have a lot of mood swings: Happy this minute, sad the next; angry now, excited soon. It is not abnormal. But as you grow you must understand that this life is real and things happen – pleasant and unpleasant alike. And whatever the case, you must learn to put your emotions in check. Sometimes, it is the happy, pleasant mood that makes us suspend our ability to make proper decisions. So, that too must be regulated.

Understanding your emotions is key to having a healthy sexuality, because if you don't know what emotions you are displaying per time, then you will not understand how it affects your sexuality.

The Mood Meter is a square divided into four quadrants — red, blue, green, and yellow — each representing a different set of feelings. Different feelings are grouped together on the Mood Meter based on their pleasantness and energy levels.

RED feelings: high in energy and low in pleasantness (e.g. angry, scared, and anxious)
BLUE feelings: low in energy and low in pleasantness (e.g. sad, disappointed, and lonely)

Come Tell Me Why

GREEN feelings: low in energy and high in pleasantness (e.g. calm, tranquil, and relaxed)

YELLOW feelings: high in energy and high in pleasantness (e.g. happy, excited, and curious)

Remember my story of seeing my GCE result which wasn't good and I became really sad? I was in the Blue zone. In that zone, I almost fell for a long-time sexual advance. For some, it's when they are excited, as in the case of parties (Yellow zone); or when they are worried, as in the case of lack and want (Red zone); or even calm and relaxed after an achievement (Green zone), that they are at their lowest resistance. You really need to be careful, and be self-aware.

Below is the Mood Meter as formulated by Yale University in America. You can print a copy for yourself and hang it somewhere easily visible, as a reminder that you are emotionally intelligent when you deliberately come out of a zone and enter into the one you need per time.

Come Tell Me Why

Ecstatic	Elated	Thrilled	Blissful	**R**	Fulfilled	Grateful	Carefree	Serene
Motivated	Inspired	Optimistic	Proud	**E**	Content	Chill	Relaxed	Tranquil
Upbeat	Cheerful	Lively	Joyful	**T**	At Ease	Secure	Satisfied	Restful
Surprised	Hyper	Energized	Pleasant	**E**	Blessed	Humble	Calm	Relieved
M	**O**	**O**	**D**	**M**	**E**	**T**	**E**	**R**
Shocked	Restless	Annoyed	Peeved	**D**	Ashamed	Apathetic	Drained	Tired
Frustrated	Nervous	Worried	Uneasy	**O**	Glum	Mopey	Timid	Bored
Furious	Frightened	Apprehensive	Troubled	**O**	Disappointed	Alienated	Excluded	Down
Enraged	Livid	Fuming	Repulsed	**M**	Disgusted	Mortified	Embarrased	Alone

Maintain Your White 80

CHAPTER ten

WELCOME TO THE WHITE CLUB

Imagine you were invited by your best friend to a club party, but with a condition: you must dress all-white from head to toe. That is your pass. Any touch of another color will stop you from entry at the venue. And your friend had hyped this party so much that you hungered to attend, so you quickly went shopping to get your all-white ready. You are eager to go to the "White Club" and experience it for yourself.

Then the D-day comes and you can't wait to get there. But shortly after you enter and start to get comfortable, you sight someone inside with a tinge of black on their shirt. What will be your reaction?

While you ponder on that, this chapter is where I will show you how to get fully dressed in your all- white of purity and be able to get access into the "White Club", which is the place of your glorious destiny that God has prepared for you. Please follow carefully and enjoy this space!

Girls Corner

A lady's purity is sacred. If a man does not value or desire to protect it until marriage, he's not the one. True love honors and protects.

— Justine Mfulama

1. Purity is a process

So many of us mess up. If not by acting out, then by the thoughts that we think. And my experience tells me that if a girl doesn't get healing from her mistakes and victory over her temptations, she'll give in all the more in the future. She'll only reach out for the help she needs if she knows she's not alone and that her battle has not ruined her. So, please know that you were not born pure and you are not alone in this process. Psalm fifty-one: five says, "Surely I was sinful from birth, sinful from the moment my mother conceived me." While we may have been born innocent, we were not born pure. Purity is the process of facing down the temptations that confront us, healing from the sins we fall into, and making right choices afterward. Purity is where you are headed, not where you begin.

Welcome to the White Club

2. Purity dreams of its future

Getting caught on the boy-craze train in middle school can trap a girl into a life of neediness. And being in a dating relationship in High School (Secondary School) increases sexual temptation, according to the Medical Institute for Sexual Health. Reduce the risk – not by just saying "no" to boys, but by dreaming of an excellent future for yourself! You are free to dream of your future. Write a list of qualities you are looking for in a husband. After all, abstinence is not about not having sex; it's about waiting to have it right!

3. Purity is governed by its value

A girl who is confident in her value as a daughter of Christ will not have need to find it in a boy or giving herself to a bearded fellow in the backseat of a car. But, with eating disorders, body image issues, and Photoshop-beauty lies on the rise, a teen girl needs a lot of self-reminding that her truest beauty is found inside her heart and not in the mirror. Take time to celebrate your creation story in Psalm one-hundred-thirty-nine where the Bible records that God knit you together. You are a masterpiece created by God. This Understanding should govern your behavior.

4. Purity speaks boldly

Many teenage girls lack what social science calls "refusal skills", that is the ability to say 'no' when temptation arises. The book of James says that the tongue is a powerful tool, compared to the rudder of a ship which has the ability to move a great vessel in any direction. Learn to use your tongue to direct your life towards purity by practicing refusal skills. Simply take time to write a list of top ten comeback lines. Have fun with it and giggle. While you may or may not use these exact statements, writing this list is a powerful internal marking point that gives you permission to say 'no', as well as the confidence to do so.

5. Purity loves its Creator at any cost

While it's great to dream about the future, it should never be in expectation that God has to or must provide a husband. A girl's value does not lie in a guy, whether you are fourteen or forty. Marriage is not the ultimate goal of your life. Being in a love relationship with Christ should be – in addition to living a life of purpose. Ephesians five: thirty-two teaches us that marriage is a picture of the love that Christ has for His bride, the Church. No one paints a picture well unless they have seen and studied the original. Thus, you must understand the beauty of a true love relationship with Jesus and be willing to protect that love at any cost. This will shield you from counterfeit love advances that are unable to help you paint a picture of the love of Christ.

6. Purity embraces wise guidance

Parent-child connectedness is considered the greatest risk reducer of teen sexual activity. Add a connected mom and dad to the power of God's Spirit in them and you have a wonderful recipe for discipleship. Of course, this means you have to talk about sex, temptation, sin, pleasure, and the beauty of the marriage bed with your mom (or mom figure). You need to talk about it, so please do so.

7. Purity watches burning flames

In one community where the middle school sexual activity rate was nearly 30%, the school system created a mentoring program pairing middle school students with high school and college students who were both sexually abstinent and sober. In just a few years, the sexual activity rate was reduced to 1%. The power of older and wiser friendships is tremendous. The Bible teaches that he who walks with the wise grows wise. Please select and connect to a mentor.

- Culled from an article by Dannah Gresh[1]

Boys Corner

The Oxford dictionary defines the word 'maintain' as 'to cause or enable to continue'. This definition is relevant in this chapter because it presents some biblical guidelines to living a sexually pure life. These keys helped me as I applied them consciously.

King David affirms that he was 'conceived' and 'birthed' in sin, yet he speaks of the need to be consecrated for fulfilling God's purposes in our lives (Psalm fifty-one: five, and twenty-four: three to five). David experienced favor, attracted breakthroughs, enjoyed successes and attained victories; yet he fell into sexual sin.

Welcome to the White Club

In my younger years, I developed a liking for the military. The uniform, carriage, authority, synched-parades and, of course, the discipline. I even attempted to join the Nigerian Army, but failed. Years later, I would go on to join the British Army as a Reservist. The training was hard. Drills were most inconvenient. Rotes and routines were unavoidable. They were all endured as this was the necessary passage to wearing the uniform, and with honor (read Second Timothy two: four).

Consecration is spiritual Discipline, and Discipline is physical Consecration. The Sergeant demonstrates, you copy; repeat; then a routine is developed, and finally discipline is attained. This principle is applicable in our discussion.

Christ demonstrates; we copy His life and pattern; we practice this life and its principles; and eventually this practice becomes second nature as our spiritual muscle is developed. For a boy, it takes discipline and self-denial to maintain purity. As sexual purity is fading away from our societies today, the advent of social media and smart phones is an added complication for young people. The days of the New

Testament were not any easier. Violence was a sport and nudity a way of life. The Romans of that day were famous for their verbal and behavioral vulgarity. Thus, purity today requires discipline, just like it did back then. Dear brother, it is time to refine yourself. Purity refers to the state of being pure, whole and devoid of impurities. Consecration refers to the discipline that leads one to purity. Consecration is the vehicle that delivers purity to us.

Let your garments always be white (Ecclesiastes nine: eight) is an admonition. It was dutiful for the singers in God's temple to be arrayed in white linen garments (Second Chronicles five: twelve). Mordecai was required to wear a white garment during the occasion of his honor (Esther eight: fifteen). Christ admonished the lukewarm Laodicean Church to get from Him white clothes to cover 'the shame of their nakedness' (Revelations three: eighteen). Joshua the high priest was accused of Satan because he was dressed in filthy priestly apparel (Zechariah three: one to seven). There is something invaluable about purity and consecration!

Welcome to the White Club

The most powerful force in the universe isn't the split atom or "Thanos' glove". It is the power of a pure lifestyle. It affords boldness, focus and a life that rises above elemental distractions and concerns. Access to the full life that accomplishes impossible things in impossible places resides within this domain. Purity is a force that neutralizes evil and spreads the full extent of the grace of God. Psalm twenty-four: four summarizes this life as: 'clean hands' and 'a pure heart'. The hands are the most sociable and interactive part of the human body. In this context, they represent all sensory organs of the body. In other words, thoughts and social interactions should be censored by the word of God.

The Bible does not admonish us to empty ourselves of mental and emotional content. Rather, we are to subject our knowledge, emotions and perceptions to God. Paul, in First Timothy four: twelve, instructs Timothy to demonstrate the character of a believer in purity, among other attributes. In Chapter five: one and two, he instructs him to treat older men as fathers; younger men as brothers; older women as mothers; and younger women as sisters with all purity (NKJV).

Having a crush, fantasizing about and lusting after a female is a waste of precious time. It cannot be excused. "All purity" speaks of the motive behind your actions. The motive behind your calls, texts, chats and hugs, must be tried by the flame of "all purity". Motive is the heart of a matter and a matter of the heart. This defines your true character in any given situation.

How can this be done?

But Jesus often withdrew to lonely places and prayed (Luke five: sixteen). It was His habit. Likewise, this excellent habit will help you to maintain your white.

The starting point to maintaining your purity as a boy is to cultivate the right routine. Remember, routines are the foundation for discipline and consecration. Jesus, our perfect example, had routines that sustained His consecration. He rose up early, went to a private place, and prayed. This scripture does not state how long His

Welcome to the White Club

prayer lasted, but there are other scriptures that suggest that Christ had hourly sessions of prayer. It is essential to seek a private space where you must meet with the Father daily. I have prayed in wardrobes, at back gardens, under trees, in cars and even in toilets. Communion with God is the medication that curtails impure thoughts and lustful desires.

In summary:

- Become a camel. Camels begin and end each day on their knees. Let your first and last words each day be to God.

- Word up. Read the Bible before breakfast. It is good practice. Meditate on a verse. It will light up your mind.

- Communicate your faith. Say what you believe by the Word of God. It cleanses your mind and keeps impure thoughts out. Speak the Word always.

- Watch your feet. Be careful where you go and the company you keep. Let the Spirit guide you. All things may be lawful, but not all are helpful. Temptation is strongest in some locations.

Welcome to the White Club

- Board the right ship. Mind your relationships. Only hang out with those who love the Lord. Fellowship is key. Bad company corrupts. Good company purifies and strengthens.

- Be a servant. Give your time and talents to the kingdom. Serve in areas where you can learn.

I pray that God will grant you grace to keep your garments white so that His oil will be poured upon your head without measure.

Amen.
- Contributed by Efa Arikpo

Benefits of Purity

> How glorious and near to the angels is youth that is clean. This youth has joy unspeakable here and eternal happiness hereafter. Sexual purity is youth's most precious possession. It is the foundation of all righteousness.
>
> — Harold B. Lee

1. You get God's best gifts (i.e. enjoy the blessings of obedience).

Welcome to the White Club

2. You will be used by God. God uses vessels of honor i.e. clean vessels. Note that being available doesn't mean you are usable by God.
3. Good health; free of sexually transmitted diseases.
4. You enjoy promotion. Righteousness distinguishes and exalts anyone who upholds it.
5. Satan has no access to transfer his agents of wickedness to you.
6. You stay focused on your future and the pursuit of your purpose.
7. Your body remains in perfect shape. Your private parts won't slack (for girls). Your strength is not depleted (for boys).
8. You save yourself the troubles of the daunting weight of addiction to sex and other vices that lead to self-destruction.
9. There will be no risk of unwanted pregnancy or forced early marriage to someone you are pregnant for, neither will there be any need for committing abortions and living with the guilt that comes with it, threat to your life or emotional pains and heart break.

Welcome to the White Club

10. You enjoy the sweet-smelling fragrance that comes with purity.
11. Honor and respect from your future spouse.
12. You reign as a King or Queen, and not live like a slave.

The list is endless....

---

[1] https://dannahgresh.com/7-secrets-to-purity-for-every-teen-girl/

CHAPTER eleven
THE THREE MASQUERADES

Masquerades are culturally disguised or costumed human beings, and are usually a threat to anyone who crosses their path without their invitation or welcome. So here, I will be showing you the threats to your quest for sexual purity which you must earnestly guard against.

A threat is usually urgent and harmful. To counter it, you have to act quickly, strategically and knowledgeably. Usually, if you are not prompt to avert a threat or stop it from taking you out, you cheaply fall prey to its intended harm.

The following are threats to your desired sexual purity lifestyle that you must wittingly guard against, with the help of the Holy Spirit:

1. Internet

The internet is inter-connected network providing a variety of information and communication facilities, a spring of knowledge and information which is required for advancement and progress in all aspects of life. The world has gone global, and that has been made possible because of the internet. The benefits of the internet cannot be exhausted; however, it came with many down sides. We have heard stories of Teenagers who met strangers on the internet and ended up getting violated, maimed or killed by them. We have also heard of people who ridicule their ex-boyfriends or ex-girlfriends and destroy their reputation in the process.

My simple advice to you is: don't surf the internet aimlessly. Always have a purpose for going there, and stick to the plan. You don't have to click everything and anything that comes up on your screen.

One of the greatest threats to your healthy sexuality, which has worsened with the advent of internet and technology, is pornography. Pornography is the portrayal or display of sexually provocative imagery (still or motion) for the purpose of sexual stimulation or lure. Pornography may be presented in a variety of media, including books, magazines, postcards, photographs, sculpture, drawing, painting, animation, sound recording, film, video, and video games. (Please take note of all these media to guard against them).

A few years ago, I was at a Secondary School in Abuja, Nigeria to do a talk for the girls on addictions. When we finished, a pretty, young SS1(Senior Secondary 1) girl ran after us to say she was addicted to pornography and was losing concentration in school. Every time her teacher was teaching, all she saw were the porn scenes playing in her head. She asked us to help her because her grades were falling and she was doing poorly in school.

Aside poor academic performance for students, pornography has other effects. The major problem is that it attacks your mind and thoughts by leaving those explicit images on it. Long after your eyes have looked at pornographic pictures, you still see them in your mind. Then your mind is programmed, leading to masturbation and a hunger to practice what you have seen on someone.

Pornography has become a very serious threat to sexual purity amongst the 21st Century teenagers, and you must fight it vigorously.

Here are some facts about Pornography you should know:

1. Males are more likely to struggle with pornography than women, hence they should make extra effort to avoid the temptation of watching it at all. Begin by ensuring you go online with a purpose, and not aimlessly.

2. Students who sleep late (not reading) are more likely to get involved with pornography than those who sleep earlier.
3. Students who fool around with friends, hang out late, and argue or fight often are more than twice likely to consume online pornographic materials.
4. The more one uses pornography, the lonelier he or she becomes.
5. People's brain might shrink or alter the more they watch pornography. It shuts down productivity.
6. There is no harmless pornographic material; everyone is potentially addictive.

However, there is hope; because you can break free from porn addiction if you want to. Here's how:
- Get off the internet or gadget(s) you use for some time.
- Discard the hardcopy materials.
- Delete the apps you watch or access them from.
- Get an accountability partner to join you on the journey to breaking free.
- Speak out. Secrecy is the environment that breeds addictions and wrong acts.
- Change your friends; because most youths were introduced to pornography by their friends.

The Three Masquerades

- Find something worthwhile to do to fill that time you use to view pornography. Remember there is no vacuum in life.
- Engage in sport and other activities that help teens to dispense their energy positively.
- Ask God for help to truly break free. Keep pleading the blood of Jesus. And when He does help you, never return to it.

2. Ungodliness

This means a lack of reverence for God and a life of holiness in the world; carelessness towards the observance of the laws of God and performance of religious duties. The ungodly person is not interested in what God's will is; not interested in making Him famous. There is no love and reverence for God and His commands.

In Genesis six: one to ten, we understand that only Noah was righteous in his day. The Lord observed the extent of human wickedness on the earth and saw that everything they thought or imagined was consistently and totally evil. It was so bad that because of this height of ungodliness, evil beings from the spirit world came down to desire and marry pretty women on earth. They

The Three Masquerades

had sexual intercourse and gave birth to giant beings. This height of immorality attracted God's anger, which led to the destruction of the then earth by flood.

Today, we make deliberate effort to push God out of our world and lives, as individuals. We see God as old-school, distant and slow. And the more we do this, the more the rate of immorality increases in our societies.

Truth is, it is difficult to have a healthy sexuality or maintain sexual purity without God, because He alone can empower us to kill the desires of the flesh, which is what fights us and keeps us from purity.

Teenagers use the term "fresh" for a really cool peer (guy or girl), because they have an outward beauty, and act in an admirable way. But the real "fresh" One is God Himself, and you who decides to live a life of holiness inside and out. Fresh is for newness, cleanliness, spotlessness. Therefore, when next you choose to use that phrase, consider it deeply.

If you must make a difference in your generation, you must make God, and your relationship with Him a priority. Carefully observing and obeying His commandments will cause His presence to abide with

The Three Masquerades

you and help you to live a holy life. He will give you the ability, grace, wisdom to stay away from sexual sin.

First Thessalonians four: three to five says, God's will is for you to be holy, so stay away from all sexual sin. Then each of you will control his own body and live in holiness and honor – not in lustful passion like the pagans who do not know God and His ways.

2. Family Disconnection

When you were a baby, you were probably mummy's boy or daddy's girl. But as you grew older, seeking independence, you gradually began to drift. You and your parents continually have fights, fights over every single thing, both small and big. And even though you act like you don't care, it hurts you much that you do not have a close relationship with your parents. Your greatest challenge is probably that your parents don't understand you, they don't trust you, they yell at you, blame you for everything, and compare you with others. All that, and maybe more, have caused you to give up on your relationship with your parents. You have a feeling your parents don't love or care for you. For the record, that is not true – I can tell you that for free!

One day, while having a discussion with a group of Teenagers, I asked how many times their parents told them

The Three Masquerades

they loved them. Some said it was yearly (probably on their birthday). Some said when they were leaving for school every term. Some said once in a while. Others said they couldn't remember how long ago. But the majority screamed: "never!"

There is also another category of Teens the Bible calls "left alone". That means their parents are alive but there is no family. Father is here, mother is there, and children are on their own; no relationship, no connection, no supervision... just alone to do whatever they like. They can leave home, move into a friend's house and stay there for days, weeks, or months, and no one will care enough to even know where they are.

In such situation, the aim of parental influence is defeated and sexual purity is highly threatened. If you are in this category, don't be thrilled at your perceived status of "freedom"; rather, be concerned and do all you can to subject yourself to a father or mother figure. What we call "freedom" can be really dangerous. I believe strongly that every child is not a child only to the people who birthed them. You can have other wonderful parents. Queen Esther was an orphan, but raised by a cousin, and rose to become a Queen who is celebrated till this day by the Jews.

Beware of these threats, dear one!

CHAPTER twelve

AFTER THE RAIN

Many Teenagers don't like to think deeply about risks and consequences. Well, that doesn't stop them from suffering them nonetheless, once you breach their conditions. As is often said, ignorance is not an excuse before the law. So, God's people perish because they lack knowledge. Sexual sin brings shame, because Sin is a sinker. It is time to understand how premarital or illicit sex affects you. We'll start with the Male Teen:

How illicit sex affects the Male Teen:

1. There is a king in every man, because men carry the mandate of authority and a mantle of leadership, wealth and strength. Hebrews one: eight(b) — A scepter of righteousness is the scepter of Your kingdom. Your scepter is your symbol of authority. That means righteousness is what secures your throne and office in life as a man.

But a stray woman can make you lose focus, just like Samson in the Bible. So, it's possible that people can be hailing you as king whereas you have lost the main

After the Rain

essence of your kingship and there is no power in your words. Proverbs thirty-one: three — "...dishonor shall he get". And what is a man without honor? Honor, respect and dignity sits well on a man, you know.

Pastor Ezekiel Atang once wrote, on the effect of sexual immorality on men: "You are reduced to bread, and bread is a consumable food, very accessible, easily. Look at Samson, a great destiny brought down cheaply, taken out without stress."

Proverbs six: twenty-six — For by means of a whorish woman a man is brought to a piece of bread: and the adulteress will hunt for his precious life.

Proverbs six: thirty-two further confirms that you destroy your own soul which is made up of your mind. Your mind is what you use to create, plan, make constructive decisions, and think critically. (Little wonder why some guys do certain foolish things and, in Nigeria we, call them *"mumu"* or *"woman wrapper"*. That's a way of saying they have lost their senses). Oops!

1. It leaves you without a defense, easily attacked. That is why you see someone who is doing so well in their

After the Rain

academics, career, or business, and suddenly things start falling apart. The hedge is broken. "Only do not rebel against the LORD, and do not be afraid of the people of the land, for they will be like bread for us. Their protection has been removed, and the LORD is with us. Do not be afraid of them!" — Numbers fourteen: nine.

2. You lose your strength. Do not spend your strength on women (Proverbs thirty-one: three). Sex requires enormous strength from the man; that is why God made him stronger. But you shouldn't spend it on any woman who is not your wife. This strength is physical, emotional, and even financial. As a Teen boy, you should learn how to earn money and invest it, not waste it on girls by trying to impress them.

3. God forgives you, but something is lost. For King David it was the son from his sinful act with Bathsheba. For some today, it is loss of their precious destiny.

"The Lord forgives you; you will not die. But because you have shown such contempt for the Lord in doing this, your child will die."
— Second Samuel twelve: fourteen.

After the Rain

Yes, God forgave you, but the scars from your escapades sometimes cling to you for life, as in the case of having a child.

There are lots more, but let me say to you boys, the world kind of exempts or subtly excuses you for being immoral. Maybe because you cannot become pregnant. But you must understand this: while you are congratulating yourself for having sex with a girl you have been chasing for a long time, you are losing even more. The book of Proverbs warns the men so much about avoiding sexual sin. It even says it can lead you to hell. Her house is the way to hell, descending to the chambers of death. (Proverbs seven verse twenty-seven).

This point is not meant to play down on you as a boy if you are being sexually harassed or molested. It is for those who willingly choose to have sex before marriage. For those being harassed sexually, I hope you can find help. Please speak to someone you trust about it.

How illicit sex affects the Female Teen:

After the Rain

1. You become a dung yard. Remember, ladies are on the receiving end during sex. So, every Tom, Tim and T empty themselves into you, sowing seeds the Bible calls 'tares'. No matter the love he professes, a man who is not your husband demanding sex from you is an enemy, because he is going against God's will for you. Soon, your true personality and essence for life is lost. We need to know the real you, darling!

2. You lose your natural sweet fragrance that God put inside you for your husband (the groom). Songs of Solomon four: eleven says, "Your lips, my bride, drip honey; Honey and milk are under your tongue, and the fragrance of your garments is like the fragrance of Lebanon." Do you know that the fragrance referred to in this scripture carries favour? That is why God says your husband will marry you and find favour. You may have noticed that some ladies are always hated, lacking favour; that could be the reason.

3. Romans six: sixteen says, "Do you not know that if you continually surrender yourself to anyone to do his will, you are slaves of whom you obey?" As a girl, you are enslaved when you give your body to a man who is not your husband. That is why even if he treats you like trash, you find yourself staying put. Premarital Sex makes you lose

After the Rain

Sex makes you lose your sense of right judgement and freedom. That's a terrible place to be.

4. You lose your favour. Every woman is endued with favour that must be activated by purity. Esther's contemporaries who also ran for the office of the Queen were virgins, but probably not pure. They did whatever they wanted. But Esther did only what her coach, Hegai (a similitude of the Holy Spirit to us) asked her to do. And the recommended purification tool earned her the throne. In Esther two: fifteen — When the turn came for Esther to go to the king, she asked for nothing other than what Hegai, the king's eunuch who was in charge of the harem, suggested. And Esther won the favor of everyone who saw her. There are so many suggestions these days on how to be holy; be careful.

5. You lose your worth and value in the eyes of the man who defiles you. Because Satan can never give you anything good – and not even for free. After Ammon defiled Tamar in Second Samuel thirteen: fifteen, he hated her much. That is probably why guys move from one lady to another because there is nothing more to look forward to. Ladies, please guard your sexuality. You are to be sought after, because there are treasures inside you!

After the Rain

6. Your lack of preparation by way of keeping yourself causes you to experience delay and displeasure in some aspects of your life like marriage, career, business, etc. In Matthew twenty-five: one to five, the five foolish virgins lacked oil in their lamps. Oil signifies the Holy Spirit. That means your time of singlehood is a time for spirituality, purification and preparation. Failure to do so might cause you pain in the future.

How illicit sex affects a nation:

Illicit sex is so bad that it can adversely affect an entire race, people, or generation. Our perfect example is Sodom and Gomorrah in Genesis thirteen: ten. It was originally a beautiful, plain, well-watered garden compared to the Garden of Eden. But all that was lost by fire when the sin of the people was so much that it attracted God's attention. Verses twenty and twenty-one say:

The outcry against Sodom and Gomorrah is so great and their sin so grievous that I will go down and see if what they have done is as bad as the outcry that has reached me. If not, I will know.

After the Rain

The prevailing sin there was illicit sex, fornication, and homosexuality.

Yes, we know that God promised not to destroy the earth in such manner again, but there are other ways a nation can suffer consequences for immorality. Such ways can be a dearth of great potentials – depicting natural, human and capital resources, or loss of lives and property through disasters and epidemics, etc.

On the other hand, righteousness exalts a nation. It is high time we collectively fought this ugly demon of immorality.

It is no joke!

CHAPTER thirteen

HOW PREPARED ARE YOU?

Today, we live in a world that communicates sex in almost everything. Directly or indirectly, unsolicited sexual images are shown to us. You can never really avoid them no matter how you shield yourself. So, the proper thing to do is to prepare for whatever will come your way by building skills and having a plan ahead. Teenage is a time for serious preparation, which involves purification. It is also a time to build on a solid foundation for the future ahead of you.

> God will not command us to live a life that is practically impossible. Sexual purity is not just possible, but is attainable.
> – Itz-voice

You will need the following Healthy sexuality skills:

A. Self-Control: the ability to control or restrain oneself, particularly one's emotions and desires, especially in difficult situations.

B. Self-Confidence: a feeling of trust in one's abilities, qualities, and judgment, including admiring and being content with one's looks.

After the Rain

C. Self-Discipline: the practice of training yourself to do what is right every time, with or without supervision.

D. Integrity: the quality of being honest and having strong moral principles. Standing for what is right against all odds.

E. Accountability: the <u>fact</u> of being <u>responsible</u> for what you do and <u>able</u> to give a <u>satisfactory reason</u> for it. It means answerability, blameworthiness, account- giving.

F. Refusal skills: a set of skills designed to help you avoid participating in risky behavior. Example, how to say 'No' and mean it, walking away amidst mockery, say 'No' without feeling bad, etc.

Make a Purity Plan

A purity plan is a detailed proposal of what you plan to do to be free from immorality, especially of sexual nature.

Making a Purity Plan is like setting an alarm clock to wake you up. Do you set it after you wake up? In other words, make your plan in advance. Always have a ready answer before the situation presents itself. Check this out for example (it can be for both boys and girls):

After the Rain

- "If you love me, you will have sex with me." Answer: "If you really love me, you will not pressure me for sex."

- "You are the only one I will ever love." Answer: "Good. That means we will have lots of time later to do whatever we want, after we marry."

- "If you don't want to have sex with me, I will find someone who will."

  Answer: "That's your choice. My choice is not to have sex."

Having said so, you need to go a step further and get a Purity Plan. And as you do, please note the following:

You need to write it down as your standards and enforce them to yourself. Don't depend on anyone else to. Hold yourself accountable and responsible first.

After the Rain

The table below is just to give you ideas; please come up with what best suits you.

1.	Do not stay with a lady or guy alone in private. Do not visit the opposite sex unaccompanied by a trusted friend. Meet only in public places and state clearly that you do not welcome surprise visits
2.	Bounce your eyes away. Do not hold a guy's gaze for too long. Do not look at a lady twice.
3.	Accepting gifts must be done with extreme care. Not every gift is genuine and harmless, with no strings attached.
4.	Focus on talks, NOT touch; conversation, NOT contact.
5	Do not permit guys to hug and touch you as they wish (you are not a teddy bear). Avoid touching ladies unnecessarily (it can send signals.)
6	Flee! Do not think at the sight of a temptation scene. Use your legs and not your mouth.
7.	Do not buy, rent, download or watch movie/TV shows that has sexual contents, nudity or crude humor. They are triggers for lust.
	Never possess or listen to music that has sweet words or sexual contents, innuendos (remarks about something sexual), crude humor (poor taste, overly vulgar), etc.
8.	Have a plan for what you are going to do online. Do not click just anything that pops up.
9.	Have an accountability partner like a mentor, parent, teacher, senior friend and/or trusted colleague.
10.	Hide God's Word in your heart. Recite it over and over again. Pray about your sexuality and ask for God's grace to overcome when temptation comes.

CHAPTER fourteen
U-TURN

Thus far, it is my hope that this book has not been a courtroom where a judge is seeking to condemn you, but rather a heartfelt message to you, telling you that purity is possible. Have you had sex before? Have you been having or still having sex habitually? You can become a secondary virgin beginning from today; you only need to make the decision now.

Are you a Teen Mom or Dad? (i.e. a Teenager who has a child outside wedlock). You don't need to give up on yourself. No! I do not need to know what happened that led you to having premarital sex or becoming a single parent at Teen age. It could have been out of sheer ignorance, willful disobedience, curiosity, a faulty mindset, unavailable parents/guardians, or worse still, rape (I say this with much sadness). Whatever it is, I want you to flip past that page of your life right now. Step out of that darkness. Come out of that cocoon you have buried yourself in and move forward!

It is time to leave the shame, name-calling, bad-mouthing, guilt, depression, disappointment, denial, backstabbing, rejection, deep-rooted pain and regret, and just move forward. Enough of the pity party (self-pity)! It's time to have a completely new view and perspective about yourself.

Forget everyone else and focus on yourself. Only two people's opinions matter here: God's and yours. You must understand that God created you for a purpose, and that purpose must be accomplished. Inside of you is a solution the world needs to be better. Come on, let that light shine from inside you!

God's love and plan for you hasn't changed, despite your past mistakes. Genuinely confess your sin to God, ask for forgiveness, and then forsake that path. You need to understand and appreciate this so you can agree and cooperate with Him to bring out the best already in you. Remember, if you cover your sin, you will not prosper. (Proverbs twenty-eight: thirteen).

Also, you must decide to never go back to your vomit or your old ways. You are not a dog. You need to rather go further to your Creator and embrace His ways. You are Royalty.

Every morning, look in the mirror and affirm yourself:
- God loves me and has great plans for me.
- My future is in front of me and not behind me.
- I have been made a king (or queen) on this earth, and I rule in righteousness.
- It doesn't matter what has happened to me, I have hope and my future is bright.
- Everything God put inside me, I will use to make the world a better place.
- Sin will not have dominion over me.
- I can and will still make a mark on earth, because I am a star.
- I choose sexual purity because it is possible.
- And as I choose to live right, I attract favour everywhere I go.

Feel free to add more affirmations of your own. Remember, you will become and have what you say, as long as you keep at it.

Purity Code

So far, we have established the fact that God is not only interested in us abstaining from sex before or outside marriage, but He equally wants us to present our bodies to Him as an acceptable and living sacrifice. In doing so, we must obey the Purity Code, which entails protecting your gates. That is, watching what happens with your Eyes, Ears, Feet, Mind and Heart gates. You must be careful that immorality doesn't come in through these gates. Only then can you be said to live a life of sexual purity.

Purity Pledge

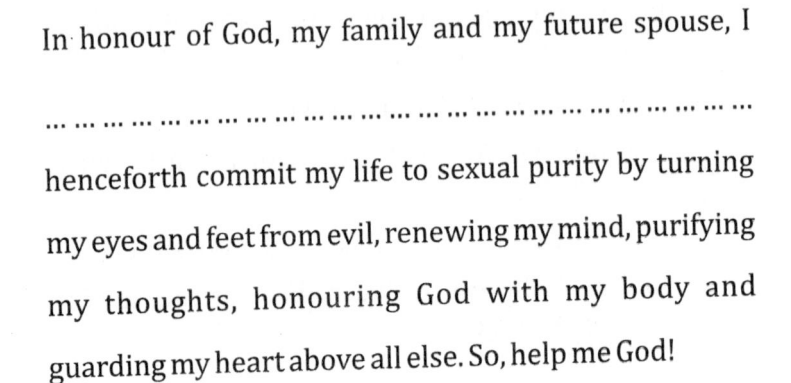

In honour of God, my family and my future spouse, I

… …

henceforth commit my life to sexual purity by turning my eyes and feet from evil, renewing my mind, purifying my thoughts, honouring God with my body and guarding my heart above all else. So, help me God!

CONGRATULATIONS!!!

CHAPTER fifteen

HEY, MOM AND DAD

Dear Mom and Dad,

Over the years, I have listened to parents express their frustrations over their children's sexuality. Usually, it's a combination of the emotions of fear, anxiety, anger, impatience, disappointment, and mistrust.

Parents usually expect a fruit from where they have not planted. Well, that sounds like magic to me. You assume that because your child is now a teenager, he or she should just know what to do and not do. My friend, Parent Coach Wendy Ologe, says, "Assumption is the lowest form of knowledge." I totally agree.

The way to get the result you desire is to have sex conversations with your child long before teenage, so that the child feels very comfortable to speak about it with you anytime. However, it should be an ongoing conversation and mostly done in an informal manner, especially utilizing what Wendy Ologe calls 'Teachable Moments'. I once heard someone say sex discussions should be like discussions on any other topic of interest in your home such as football, current affairs, etc. I

Hey, Mom and Dad

agree. If the word 'sex' sounds discomforting to your lips, I suggest you say it loudly twenty-one times so you get used to it. (LOL)

By all means, you cannot afford to be evasive, economical with words, untruthful, or worse, ignorant of the subject of sex. Imagine there was no one (friends, teachers, or the internet) to tell your child about sex, no one to answer their questions. Will what you tell your child be sufficient for him or her to live sane in this highly sexualized world we are in?

From helping your child build a healthy esteem, to developing Godly character, to sharpening decision-making skills, to rightly using the tools that aid purity, to drawing up a Purity Plan, and lots more, all lie in your hands. The good news though is that because you have come in contact with this material, you can begin now from where you are or improve on what you have done already.

Here are some points to note while bringing up a child/teen that is sexually pure.
- You must obey these three (3) laws:

(i) The Law of Connection: A wise man said, "Rules without relationship leads to rebellion." Connect with your child by being involved in their lives. You can't just show up with a list of dos and don'ts just because it's for their own good. Spend time together, do things together, talk, share, bond, have fun. All these will prepare your child to listen to your counsel.

(ii) The Law of Communication: Communication involves both talking and listening. As a parent, it's easier to talk than listen, so you must be deliberate about listening to your child. Usually, Teens will test you by telling you something that happened to them, but in the disguise that it happened to their friend. If you flare-up or show no understanding, they will shut down and bring no more information to you. Teenagers usually complain of overreactions from their parents, so you want to be careful. When they offend, correct; don't condemn!

(iii) The Law of Care: Care is showing empathy to your child. "My parents don't understand me" is the number one complain I always hear from Teens. Understand what their struggles are, their weaknesses, fears and shortcomings; that is empathy. Show them tenderness and affection. When your Teen receives much care from you, they will naturally respond positively.

- Be as straight forward and truthful as possible, revealing necessary information per time according to the age of the child. The older they are, the deeper you reveal. When you lie, today's child knows and would avoid speaking to you on that matter.
-
- One of my mentees (a 12-year-old) said to me that it's so sweet to hear a guy say he loves her. What that simply means is that she is lacking affection from her parents, especially her father. That's why she appreciates the affection from a boy who, if care is not taken, will demand a romantic relationship from her at that tender age. Who doesn't want to feel loved? Parents, please show affection to your

Hey, Mom and Dad

teenagers. Take them out to the movies, to restaurants, to parks. I do not mean family outings; I mean one on one hangouts. Dad and daughter, Mom and son, and vice versa.

- Model purity to your children. One day, I and my teenage daughter went to an event for mothers and children. As she alighted from the car, a CD in the car next to us caught her attention. It was a pornographic material. Wow! And the car owner was a parent!

  - Do you know you are the purity book your child is reading? Say what you want, but you will ultimately parent your type. So, if you have no moral values, your children will be same, if not worse. Let your life and home be free of pornographic materials and immoral scenes, songs, swear words, chaos. Fill your home with genuine love, laughter and peace, which attract God's presence and leaves your children yearning for their own homes when they're out.

Hey, Mom and Dad

- When having sex conversations with your Teens, don't paint sex as bad, painful and sinful. Emphasize that God designed sex to be beautiful and pleasurable, but only to be done on the Marriage bed. Do not change the message just because you made a mistake. Instead, let them know you made a wrong choice and if given another chance will do better. I often see parents twisting the purity message to suit us and the circumstances we find ourselves in. We are afraid our children will judge us; but we must not let them get entangled in that web. We made mistakes, because we are human; so stop acting like a super being.

- Teach contentment as a value with great gain. I have seen Teens fall into fornication and homosexuality because of greed and covetousness. For girls, we hear of "small girl, big god" where Teen girls date older men just for designer bags, shoes and money. Gadgets, phones, etc. could also be baits used in luring them (boys inclusive). They must be content with what you have provided for them. Parents, please stay awake.

Hey, Mom and Dad

- Speak positive and affirmative words that will help build, not destroy your child's self-esteem. You should tell your child how pretty they look, etc. Abusive words, foul language, mock of your child's physical looks (e.g. big head, black lips, etc.) must never be heard from your mouth. Remember, Teens are at a stage of identity crisis — not sure of who they are or if they like what they have on their bodies. You can help them through that process by affirming them. If not, you will push them over to an opposite sex outside for unhealthy indulgence.

- Every child has a 'love tank' that must be filled as they grow. You can do this by loving your child in the way he or she understands and can easily receive. The 5 love languages as stated by Gary Chapman are:

a. Physical Touch — like hugs, pats on the back, pecks, high 5's, etc.

b. Quality Time — spending time together, not necessarily how long but how well, doing valuable activities with rich content. Remember, you can be present and yet not be with them.

c. Acts of Service — helping them, but not completely taking off all their chores. Surprising them by physically doing something they should have done. This can be done often, but not always, so as not to spoil them by getting them lazy.

- Words of Affirmation— appreciating, emphasizing strengths and efforts, praising them, etc.
  - Gifts—buying them things not necessarily expensive, but useful to them.
    - Display Godly/good character. Be mindful of how you relate with the opposite sex online and offline. You are not exempted from Sexual Purity. Indulging in extramarital affairs is a terrible message to pass to your children. Remember that children learn more from what you do than what you say.
    -
  - Build Godly character in your children. Sexual purity is impossible without God. Godliness means looking like God. Thus, be mindful of your child's dressing and appearances. Sometimes, when I see some teens inappropriately dressed and speak to them, they look at me innocently and say, "My mom bought it for me."

Hey, Mom and Dad

Especially these days where our children look like overgrown babies, with all the curves in all the right places, you shouldn't encourage your child to dress in tight revealing clothes, all in the name of looking sexy, like a Mom once said when confronted.

- The internet has become part of our lives as we now live in a digital age, hence you must be involved in your child's life online. Teach, guide and supervise them on what to do when they go online. There should be rules for when they're online. For example, they should have a purpose of going online (research, information, news, training, etc.). They should know that it's wrong to chat with strangers (very common with Teens) or click on pictures and sites of pornographic nature. Ensure your child is emotionally and behaviorally ready and responsible before you give him or her a phone with unlimited access to the internet.

- Be careful not to spoil your children with expensive gifts, especially gadgets, when they are not prepared or mature for them.

Hey, Mom and Dad

- Do not expose your child to an environment or lifestyle you cannot sustain. I have seen Teenagers from average homes in schools with elite kids and after sometime begin to engage in sexual activity with them in exchange for material things, because their parents can't provide them. Do not expose them to the pressure that comes from watching others show off around them• Guide your child to find the right role models. As Teens, it is not unusual to see them admire and be fans of celebrities, music/movie stars; but you should emphasize the right values they should watch out for in role models. Imagine your child's role model is a celebrity who is a Baby-Mama or Daddy, scarcely dresses well and maybe acts wild. It will send a strong message of societal acceptability to your child.

- Don't judge or blacklist your child no matter what they have done. Constantly reminding them of their mistakes can push them back into the world. A Teen Mom told me once that after she had a baby, her parents sought every little opportunity to tell her how irresponsible, loose and flirty she was. She became depressed and went into another sexual relationship. Please do not tell her story to other family members or friends. Shaming a child is no correctional or discipline technique.

- Keep your home clear of illicit music, videos and TV programs, and let your child understand why.

- Do not use your children for trafficking, no matter how tough life gets for your family. Instead, do whatever you must — within conscience — to get out of such quagmire. I have heard the mother of a very pretty girl ask her: "Can't you use what you have to get what you need?" (The girl needed money to register for her WAEC/JAMB exam). Unfortunate!

- You need to trust your child. Trust they will do what you have taught them, what is right and what pleases God. Teenagers complain bitterly about how much it hurts them to know their parents don't trust them, i.e. when their parents always suspect them — their movements, activities and actions. This distrust can discourage them from striving for sexual purity. You should be cheering them on as they go on this journey and don't be afraid to correct them when they make mistakes.

- Studying God's Word should not be seen as old school by this generation, because it is God's Word in their heart that will keep them from sinning no matter how far they are from you. Teach them to love, read and meditate on God's Word. The world might have changed but the Word of God hasn't.

- Have a parenting library (i.e. a collection of parenting books in different areas). Dress your mind and your child's mind, preparing them for whatever the world will bring to them.

- Can you think twice before sending your teenagers to certain nations whose environment stinks of immorality, making it really tough for them to sustain their purity? I know the world has become highly sexualized, but I also know that it is worse in some societies. Schooling in another nation should not be a function of whether you can afford it, but rather the ability of your child to withstand the pressures of an ill society.

- Stop living in denial. Face the reality that your child might have already been exposed or involved in sexual activity. Do something about it instead of shouting 'God forbid!' There is no case too bad to be handled. Do not also overreact when you discover certain behaviors that don't conform; instead, calm down and counsel.

- Prayer is a force that can build a shield around your child. It keeps people with wrong motives from hurting them. Pray for and with your child. Prayer helps them overcome temptation, breaks every chain and brings victory. A praying Teenager is a victorious one. Teach them how, and exemplify a lifestyle of prayer to them.

CONCLUSION

Darling Teenager, thank you for coming on this journey with me. I celebrate you. I trust that you have been enriched and empowered to make positive and Godly changes in your life going forward, and to embrace the sweet and rewarding life of purity.

Now, I want you to know that following this path of purity is not putting yourself in prison or bondage. Obeying God and doing what is right might make you look like a fool right now, especially these days that youths feel they have a right to have sex if they choose, but the Bible says there is a way that seems right but ultimately only leads to destruction. A life of sexual impurity is a surefire path to self-destruction, with far-reaching ill consequences as we have discussed already in this book. Which would you prefer: to endure now and enjoy the glorious future God has prepared for you later, or to "enjoy" sexual sins now and live a life of pain and regrets in the future? The choice is yours, sweetheart.

There is a special and unique course for your life. Do not be afraid to follow it, because in the end you will find true love, happy marriage, and great sex. That is the sequence

Conclusion

and not the other way around. Live your life in such manner that you will bring purity to your marriage, home and children. Trust me, your future-self would eternally thank you for it. There are several practical examples and proofs to learn from, some of which I have shared in this book. Strive to do likewise.

I look back at my friends I took the purity vow with as Teenagers. They are all doing well, they got married to wonderful Godly men, they have very good jobs, children, name it! God has blessed them all-round.

Focus your mind on your future and pay the price today. And, I challenge you, rather than wait to be pressured by others, go and become a peer influencer instead – encouraging your friends to live a life of purity and chastity.

> Nothing has stolen more dreams, dashed more hopes, broken more families, and messed up more people psychologically than our propensity to disregard God's commands
> regarding sexual purity.
> — Andy Stanley

If a beautiful life of royalty is on your mind for your future, then Purity is it!

ABOUT THE AUTHOR

Etima Umeh is a Teens Mentor with nearly 20 years experience. Her purpose is to raise responsible teenagers who are balanced in all areas of life. That passion drives her to partner with parents to coach, mentor, train and build capacity amongst youths. Many of her Teens have become Peer Mentors nationwide.

She is the Lead Mentor at the Teens Roundtable Academy, Africa's biggest online life-skill school for Teens, the Convener of Responsible Teens and Mentoring Bootcamp. She is also the President of the NGO-Inspire for Greatness Network.

She is an Entrepreneur involved in Agribusiness and Consulting.

Aunty Etima, as she is fondly called, is married to Matthew Umeh and together they are blessed with 3 children.

Connect with Etima Umeh for trainings, consultancy and speaking engagements.

Facebook - Etima Umeh
Instagram - Etima Umeh
E-mail- etimaoni@gmail.com
Website- www.etimaumeh.com
Phone- +234 (0) 809 715 1511

For detail of our courses and programs.
Website-www.responsibleteensacademy.com
Facebook-Responsible Teens
Instagram-Responsible Teens